Jews, Israelis and Arabs

An Observer's View
Of Israel's Shifting Society

Shalom Pollack

Mazo Publishers

As soon as we turned our backs on our Jewish identity, we lost the ability to remain loyal to our Israeli identity as well.

... Rabbi Avraham Yitzchak Hakohen Kook

———◈———

Jews, Israelis and Arabs
ISBN: 978-1-956381016

Copyright © 2021 Shalom Pollack
E-mail: shalompollack613@gmail.com

Published by

▐▚▌

Mazo Publishers
www.mazopublishers.com
mazopublishers@gmail.com

I would like to first dedicate this book to my mother, Rosalind Pollack. Many of the ideas were distilled in deep discussions about our common love for and pride in the Jewish people, its history and culture.

I would like to thank my heroes, the brave Jews in the Land of Israel today who refuse to "go along to get along" and dare insist that "the Emperor has no clothes." They cling to the land because they cling to truth.

The pioneers of a century ago sacrificed for our land, too. They paid a personal price but were strengthened and encouraged in the knowledge that they enjoyed the admiration of their generation. The current "settlers" and "hilltop youth" pay a personal price in their dedication to the same land as did the earlier pioneers.

The difference is that the current idealists persevere despite being treated as outcasts by their own people. They do not flee social marginalization, institutional harassment, physical danger, jail or even death. In this they are like our flag bearers from time immemorial.

It is easy to adore champions of the distant past. In each generation only a few rise above the masses to become leaders and are often not recognized or appreciated during their lifetime.

I admire the true heroes of our generation. I need not wait for history books to reveal their names. From them, I draw my inspiration and desire to write this book.

Contents

Contents

Contents

Foreword

In this book, "Jews, Israelis and Arabs", Shalom Pollack describes the experience of immigration and acclimatization of a Brooklyn-born Jew in the State of Israel, and comments on current events in Israeli society.

The importance of the book is not only in the writer's personal experience, but in the insights he shares.

Understanding the intersection of identities in which Israel's society stands – the struggle between the Israeli and the Jew – we are provided with a glimpse of events to understand what is happening in Israel. For a Jew planning to immigrate to Israel (Aliyah), this book is especially important and will help to eliminate much of the confusion and doubts.

To this day, the contradiction between the aspiration of Israeli normalcy and the desire to fulfill the Jewish mission has been resolved through compromise. The most famous of the attempts is the Gavison-Medan Covenant, which sought the golden pathway, which would allow Israelis and Jews to continue to travel together on their shared journey.

It is not compromise, but synergies that we need. We need the formula for connecting the opposites, and we are making progress towards reaching this goal.

When the Israeli and the Jew will no longer fear each other, but instead, contribute to the special qualities of the other, a great opportunity will emerge from Zion and our country will be a miracle for the nations.

Moshe Feiglin
Founder of the "Zehut" movement,
Former Member and Speaker of the Israeli Knesset

Introduction

When Shimon Peres lost the election to Benjamin Netanyahu in 1996, he was asked, "Who lost?"
He answered, "The Israelis."
"And who were the victors?"
"The Jews."

As an observer of Israel and Jewish history, I notice an accelerating battle for the identity of the Jewish state.

When I first visited and then moved to Israel, I was certainly aware that some Israelis were more "religious" than others, just as in the US.

Unlike in the US, I believed that in Israel it was considered natural and a source of pride for all Israelis to identify as Jews.

In the US, without a minimal Jewish education, the path to assimilation is certain.

In Israel, Hebrew is the language spoken by everyone. Most serve in the army where all share the same tent.

I was aware that many Israelis did not follow all of the Torah but I was impressed that they studied "Tanach" (Torah scriptures) in school and had a proud connection to the land. This can be possible only in a Jewish country. Israelis can read holy texts with the same ease as a newspaper. Amazing!

Politicians, lawyers, writers and others quote from our sacred texts. This familiarity with the holy words reflects a national spirit albeit, not a familiarity with the synagogue.

I moved to Israel in 1977 after visiting and studying there on earlier occasions. Looking back, it seems that my first exposure came at a significant turning point in Israeli society.

The founding generation of secular Zionists had a relationship with the classic texts and were proud of their Jewish literacy. However, they did not pass on the little "Yiddishkeit" they retained from the "old country" to their children. The fathers were proud Jews but the next generations became disconnected and ignorant of things Jewish.

One of the major Zionist figures of the Left, Yaakov Hazan

lamented, "we intended to raise a generation of informed apostates but they are in fact ignorant of that which we wanted them to reject."

The term "a state of all its citizens" was one that I heard of years ago. It was an idea batted around in the political margins of the Left. Compromising the Jewish character of the state for the inclusion of non-Jews was the goal. "Pluralism," "self-realization" and "minority rights" are sacred values for the Left.

The very concept of a Jewish state is ipso facto discriminatory to non-Jews and thus the Jewish state was born in sin. It was a mistake that needs fixing.

Israel faces a decision – Jew or "Israeli?"

What is the relationship of Israel to the ancient and revered values of Jews? What is the identity of the Jewish state called Israel?

Identity is the key word.

The Left likes to talk about a "democratic – Jewish state" where democratic overrides Jewish.

What is the famous "two thousand years dream" one hears about often? Is it next year in a Jewish Jerusalem or perhaps in a Jerusalem where any person can claim a part and feel equally at home in a cosmopolitan city?

What is the essence of the words "Zion" and "Zionism?" Is it democracy that demands the deconstruction of Judaism?

Is that the Jewish ideal?

Or is it the call for Jews to fulfill a dream of generations past and future?

It is my observation that the Left is less concerned with democratic and more concerned with not Jewish.

How do I know? Some examples:

- Unabated antipathy for the "settlers" who dare remind us of the unbreakable biblical ties to our land.

    The demographic argument of the Left that Israel must not extend its sovereignty to all parts of our land rings hollow when they lobby for the tens of thousands of illegal African infiltrators and foreign workers whose visas expire to receive citizenship, or when they want to bring to Israel tens of thousands of

Arabs to "unite" with Israeli Arab marriage partners. How does this square with their concern of the "loss of the Jewish majority" and thus the emergency need to relinquish our land?

- Negating the traditional Sabbath in the public sphere, which symbolizes and unites the Jewish people from time immemorial.

- Denying Jewish children in public schools the most basic concepts of Judaism and raising yet another generation of Jewish illiterates.

- The campaign to encourage the destruction of the Jewish family.

The list is long.

This is not the same Left that I met during my early visits to Israel. There is a struggle today for the identity of this country that I did not notice when I first visited in 1971.

The challenge of Israeli Arabs is but a symptom of the unsettled question of our own identity.

For many on the Left, Arab physical attacks on the country are less a concern to them than "Jews" leading "their" country.

Many of the articles that I have written over the years and included in this book record the change in Israeli politics and society as reflected in events that I witnessed.

I realized that there are those in positions of power who simply do not want a Jewish country. This was an unthinkable suggestion when I first arrived.

If they lived in the USA, these Jews would simply assimilate. Here it is more complicated. Often the children of the founding fathers, they see themselves as nobility with wealth and power that they do not want to abandon.

Still, many do leave the country. Their numbers in Israel are waning as they have smaller families than the "Jews" and "alternate lifestyles" are becoming more commonplace.

In their desperation for power, they openly court anti-Zionist Arab parties to share what little public support they still have. This was taboo for their fathers, but now ignored by them as they desperately cling to power and influence.

The Israeli Arabs who lost the war of 1948 still mourn that defeat. It was an illusion to think that Israel's Arab citizens would accept Jewish national domination and become happy partners.

Their history, religion, education and culture do not allow for acceptance of defeat by Jews. Civil liberties and material benefits do not compensate for the feeling that we took their honor, their land, and their (imagined) country. On the contrary, each concession to them is seen as weakness, not as kindness or a sense of justice.

Their demands and gripes will never end as long as there is a Jewish state. They demand a "state of all its citizens," as do the Left.

Of course, the Left does not realize that the Arabs won't stop there and will not be satisfied until they win their Arab "Palestine" back.

Our Jewish state faces many challenges, the greatest of which is for the identity of the country; how we define ourselves. Once our identity as a Jewish country and people is established; once the "who" and "why" is clear, the "how" will proceed.

It is my hope that this book, which is an accumulation of decades of observations and study of Israel and its people, will contribute to this process.

The first articles reflect a very general picture of Israel and its society from the vantage point of my personal experiences including as a father, a professional tour guide, and a reserve soldier in the "people's" army, that is an army that has representations from all walks of Israeli life.

The bulk of the articles try to explain the intra-Jewish relationships which ultimately orbit around the key subject of the book and that is how to define a Jewish identity in the Jewish state.

The final articles deal with the relations between the Jewish state and the Arabs beyond and within our borders and thoughts on possible paths of action.

SP

Background

This book is about Israel. My personal observations and thoughts as I have closely observed over the years are reflected in the articles included.

In order to better understand the discussion and terms used in this book, an introduction to the country, the land, its people and history is helpful.

To make a 4,000-year story short –

The Bible tells us that the people of Israel and the land of Israel were chosen by God for each other and for Him. The Israelites began to form as a people beginning with Abraham 4,000 years ago, culminating with Moses and the Exodus from Egypt with receiving the Torah on Mount Sinai 3,500 year ago.

After Moses' passing, Joshua led the Israelites into the promised land 3,450 years ago and conquered it from the Canaanites as commanded by God.

King Solomon built the First Temple on Mount Moriah (Temple Mount) in Jerusalem 3,000 years ago. It was destroyed by the Babylonians 2,500 years ago and the Israelites were exiled to Babylon. Seventy years later, King Cyrus of Persia conquered Babylon and allowed the Jews to return to Israel and rebuild the Second Temple in Jerusalem. That temple was destroyed by the Romans almost 2,000 years ago and most of the Jews were exiled from Israel.

A small remnant remained and was faithful to the Torah during the harsh Roman and then Byzantine rule. The Jewish presence was greatly reduced, though not eliminated, with the Moslem conquest in the 7th century. Jews continued to live in the land, especially in the ancient biblical cities.

Great destruction and suffering came with the Crusades in the 11th and 12th centuries, yet some Jews still clung to the land.

Small but important centers of Jewish scholarship flourished during the years of Moslem occupation.

Change began in the 19th century with emancipation and nationalism in Europe. Centuries of Jewish longing to leave the exiles and return to their homeland was given political form with the Zionist movement led by Theodor Herzl. He succeeded in galvanizing the imagination and hope of the Jewish masses throughout the exiles as concrete plans were discussed for the return home.

Jews began to return in small numbers to a land that was anything but the longed for biblical land of "milk and honey. "

As Mark Twain put it when he visited, "even the grasshopper got hungry there." It was a very underpopulated land that no one invested in – and for good reason.

Idealistic Jewish pioneers took up the challenge and eventually the neglected land returned its love and blessing to them. The prophecies of the greening of the deserts came true. The ingathering of the exiles, another prophecy, was unfolding as well. The Talmud tells us that these two prophecies fulfilled are the clearest signs the Messianic period has arrived.

In 1917, Britain issued the "Balfour Declaration" which declared their support for a Jewish homeland in "Palestine." (Palestine was the name given by the Romans when they tried to erase any memory of Jewish ties to the land.) Jews throughout the world were jubilant about this important British recognition and support.

The League of Nations endorsed the right of the Jews to their country in the 1920 San Remo conference. The British, who were given the mandate to carry out the 1920 decision, reneged on their responsibility. They withdrew their support for the Zionist endeavor and favored Arab opposition to Jewish immigration and settlement.

In 1922, the British gave away all the land east of the Jordan to the Hashemite dynasty from Arabia and created for them a country in land that was allocated for the Jews by the world community and Britain herself.

During the Holocaust, the British sealed the borders of Palestine and sent many thousands of Jews back to their deaths in Europe.

In 1947, the UN voted to partition what remained of Palestine into a Jewish state and a second Arab one (the first was created in 1922 on the eastern side of the Jordan river).

The proposed Jewish state was far smaller than the one promised by the League of Nations in 1920 but the Jews agreed to take what they could.

The Arabs rejected all compromises (they were offered a generous compromise in 1936 – the Peel Commission which they also rejected) and threatened the destruction of the Jews.

In 1948, Jewish underground forces finally expelled the British. When the last of the British left on May 14, 1948, the Arab countries and those within attacked the tiny Jewish community of 600,000 people (the same number as those who left Egypt during the Exodus).

To the world's surprise, Israel won the war and expanded the partition borders. Many Arabs fled the fighting and became refugees in neighboring Arab countries. The refugees were supported in facilities run by the UN and were restricted by their host Arab countries.

The Arabs who remained in Israel enjoyed full citizenship.

In 1967, the Arab world decided again to eliminate the Jewish state. In the Six-Day War, Israel defeated a coalition of Arab armies and won yet more of the biblical promised land.

Since then, Israel gave the Sinai back to Egypt for peace (1977). Part of this treaty included the uprooting of thousands of Jews from communities in Sinai. This was a precursor to similar expulsions of Jews from their homes as part of a political calculation.

In 1993, Israel's Left government, led by Yitzchak Rabin and Shimon Peres, invited Yasser Arafat, the head of the PLO terror organization to the heartland of Israel in the hope that he would agree to live in peace and "end the conflict."

Arafat was given large chunks of the biblical heartland won in the 1967 war. The Oslo Accords gambled that he would be satisfied with these concessions. He was not, and it did not "give us peace."

Arab terror increased many fold as Arafat was armed by Israel, granted authority and land to form the "Palestinian Authority."

Israel gave Gaza to the Arabs in 2005, which the Hamas terror group promptly took control of.

In the process of these concessions, many thousands of Israelis were expelled from their homes and their land was given to Arabs, mainly the Gush Katif "expulsions for peace and security."

It did not work. Gaza became a terror center plaguing Israel to this day.

My writings are the result of close observation of Israel, especially in the "post Oslo" period, but not exclusively.

I share insights into life in a unique country, famously influenced by politics and in constant danger.

Israel is the only country and people today facing genocide; this after an attempt not long ago.

Israel is a biblical prophecy in the making. It is the story of the impossible happening, at times despite ourselves. It is where, as Ben Gurion said, "if you don't believe in miracles, you are not a realist."

It is this Israel that I made my home and pray for.

Shalom Pollack
2021

A Great Man Prophesied

Rabbi Avraham Yitzchak Hakohen Kook found himself at the center of continuing controversy as chief rabbi of Eretz Yisrael. He was an original thinker and revolutionary in his synthesis of the values of the Land of Israel, the people of Israel and the Torah of Israel. In his tumultuous time, the Jewish world was divided into numerous and distinct camps.

Many identified with the Torah, but the concept of the Jewish people as a nation with land was at best a faded memory. Community survival against the threats of a menacing world was their sacred mission.

As the modern era and emancipation began, the idea of a Jewish nation and Jewish land was revived among some Jews. Other Jews, especially in the West, embarked on a reformation of the faith.

Some Jews, mainly in Russia, saw purpose and salvation in world movements such as Socialism and Communism. Others, in lands where emancipation held promise, clung to a grudging acceptance and were determined to prove their worth as equals and patriots.

Some, in Eastern Europe, stressed Jewish secular culture that revolved around the Yiddish culture and Jewish socialism.

Some stressed the humanitarian and cosmopolitan mission of Judaism. Still, others solved the dilemma – through the church.

Jewish history found itself at a crossroads. Two movements emerged from the turmoil as the champion claimants and vied for leadership of the next phase of Jewish history.

The Agudah movement and allies in the "old country" fiercely defended the status quo. What was, must be. Ideas of a sovereign Jewish nation, land, or people were simply seen as yet another threat.

Then there were the Zionists who rebelled against what was,

and sought a "new Jew," sovereign and proud in his own country, working and defending the land, speaking his own language.

In rejecting the status quo of a dehumanizing Diaspora, they cut their ties to the one thing that assured Jewish existence during the long dark exile. A Jewish nation and land, but without Torah, was their vision. No longer would the Jewish people be a nation that dwelt alone, but a "normal" one, accepted by the family of peoples. They would be just like them.

The two camps glared at each other from distant corners.

Unlike much of the rabbinic world, Rabbi Kook had a great appreciation for the young idealistic pioneers and dreamers. He shared a part of that same dream. He dedicated himself to working with them, while trying to teach them why the Torah had to be a part of their vision.

Rabbi Kook drew harsh criticism from the rabbinic establishment. How could a rabbi associate with sinners and scoffers?

Rabbi Kook responded to them in a famous letter in which he asked them, "Who tries to teach them if not me?" In another letter, he turned to his pioneer friends and made a dire prediction. He warned them that if they continued to be divorced from the Torah, their children would reject the very Land of Israel for which they dedicated themselves.

He proved to be a prophet.

Am Yisrael (The Nation of Israel)

It was my third year of college and I was an exchange student from Brooklyn College in Brooklyn, New York. At that point of my life after some visits, I sought any excuse to be in Israel. A year of study was perfect.

Of course, that year was not to be anything as planned when the 1973 Yom Kippur war broke out at the beginning of the first semester. What I missed out on in class was compensated for in life experiences and a unique chance to bond with my people and land traumatized by a war that was almost lost.

We students were asked to volunteer in various places as Israeli men were in the reserves for extended periods. I was exposed to new places and people.

The experience I remember most was when I was sent to Moshav Yardena.

Moshav Yardena is a farming community in the Upper Jordan Valley along the banks of the Jordan River (thus the name Yardena). It is populated by Jews from Kurdistan, the rugged and isolated mountains of northern Iraq. Their history is fascinating. They were probably remnants of the "ten lost tribes" who managed to hold on to Judaism from time immemorial. In Kurdistan, they were farmers and were not known for a scholastic tradition.

When they immigrated to Israel after the state was established, they continued farming and were also laborers, especially in the building trade.

In the early years of the state, immigrants were often sent to populate outlying or border areas that needed a Jewish presence. Thus, Yardena was born.

It remained relatively isolated physically and from the mainstream of Israeli culture as well. When I arrived, the younger generation was in a period of "transition" between the old and the new.

After a combination of long bus rides and hitchhiking, I finally arrived. I walked along the empty quiet main road leading up to the moshav wondering who was supposed to greet me. When I finally did see people, they stared at the stranger struggling with the heavy backpack looking very lost.

In my poor Hebrew I must have said something like, "take me to your leader." They were puzzled. They did not know what I wanted.

I finally met a younger person who understood English and I explained that I was sent to volunteer.

Volunteer? With which family? To do what? It dawned on me that no one was aware of my great mission.

Eventually, I was seen as a needy traveler and it would not be honorable to just send me away. I was shocked and disappointed that no one was told of my coming and that apparently, I was not needed.

As long as I was there, enjoying their hospitality, I said I would like to work. They obliged and I joined some young people working in the cotton fields. At one point it began to rain. No panic. No rush. We all just sat under the wagon and watched the rain until it stopped. Life in the fields was new to me.

I was delighted when I was invited to stay for Pesach. I realized that none of them had ever spoken to an American before, and I had never met a Kurdish Jew. It was going to be an unusual Pesach for me.

We sat around the seder table and discussed the Egyptian Exodus as they did in Kurdistan, as I did in Brooklyn. At that seder table I gained a new appreciation of the term "Am Yisrael."

My experience amongst the embracing Kurdish Jews of Yardena was yet another deciding factor for my making Aliyah a few years later.

Chanukah Diary

After a three-month stay in the US, I returned to Israel during Chanukah in 1990. The country was grappling with the first intifada (Arab uprising). It was also when the Gulf crisis had erupted. Much of my time in the States was actually focused on news about Israel during this tense period. I assumed that the news coverage about the events and the mood in Israel did not present the true picture. It was never as bad as that painted by the media.

With this in mind I boarded a plane that would take me home. The absence of tourists on the flight reminded me that I was not going to have much work as a guide when I returned. With only Israelis seated around me, I realized how isolated from the world Israel was at this time.

When I landed at Ben Gurion, I realized just how quickly things were changing for my adopted country.

An "Aeroflot" plane rested on the tarmac as we landed. A Russian plane in Israel would have been surprising enough. The hundreds of Russian Jews that it brought was truly history in the making; prophetic. As they arrived, they were each given a gas mask to protect them from Saddam Hussein's threats to gas Israel. It did not seem to perturb them. They were happy to be home.

Who would have imagined this scene just a year ago!

Upon entering the newly constructed arrivals complex, built to accommodate the nonexistent tourism boom, it was now greeting a massive Russian Aliyah. Who said that God does not have a plan?

I tried not thinking about the challenges of housing and absorbing so many of our brothers and sisters. Just processing them upon arrival was a huge challenge. I was confident. Was there a choice?

Riding in the taxi to Jerusalem, my thoughts about Israel's destiny were interrupted by the driver's cheers as his favorite basketball team scored. Jerusalem's team beating Haifa. Hurray!

The driver focused on what was really important in life. Why worry?

First candle of Chanukah:

Shopping for food brought me back to the real world. Once again, I wonder just how they (we) do it? Food costs about twice as much as in the US. A gallon of gas is almost three times the price. A Honda Accord costs $50,000 in Israel. It is $15,000 in the US. The sales tax was just raised to 18%.

No protests or outrage. Israelis buy food and fill their tanks and go on. The looming threat of Saddam Hussein's missiles does not seem as concerning as my turn to pay at the checkout counter.

The cabinet ministers are at it again. Public posturing, insults; the ego wars go on. Politics as usual.

Suddenly all of our concerns and gripes vanish as the radio announces another victim of the intifada – a young soldier was murdered. Another funeral. We are reminded that we are one family.

As I light the first Chanukah candle with my family and thank God for the miracles of this time and this place, I pray, "please don't stop now."

Second candle:

The note my son brought home from school read, "the third grade is going to visit a reconstructed Maccabean village. Parents with personal weapons are requested to accompany us."

In which other country do Jewish children visit a Maccabean village; and where else are parents asked to ride shotgun? I volunteered, though I did not then own a weapon. As it turned out, it was only me and a mom (a travel agent also out of work at the time), who volunteered.

So, there I was baking pita bread over an open fire and making clay oil lamps with these young heirs of the Maccabees in the land of the Maccabees.

Our young Yemenite guide enthusiastically made it all come alive in that village not far from where the dramatic events took place over two millennia ago. What a thought.

Little Alek, newly arrived from Russia, hung on to every one of the guide's words. I asked him, "How is Israel different from Russia?"

Squinting into the winter sun, he said that he remembers crying from the severe cold in Leningrad.

On the bus, I overheard two children talking. "You know what I am really afraid of?" I'm afraid of Arabs attacking our bus."

For the rest of the ride, the boys looked out the window trying to identify Arab villages along the road. What would a Maccabean government do to allay the fears of these children?

Third candle:

Prime Minister Yitzchak Shamir met with President Bush (senior) in Washington. The meeting went well – to everyone's relief.

The American president actually allowed himself to be seen in public with an Israeli leader even as he was putting together the grand Arab coalition against Iraq. The one thought Arabs find more threatening than Iraqi invasion is Jews.

Russian leader Shevardnadze had a well-publicized meeting with Shamir. Things were looking promising for a moment.

A knife wielding Arab wounded a soldier and a passerby as the latter came to the soldier's aid. The Arab was wrestled down by other citizens. The hero was interviewed on TV and was asked if he would do the same in the future? With an incredulous look, he said, "Of course, what else could I do?" I compared this attitude with the typical New Yorker. I was happy that I was home.

Fourth candle:

Rain, rain, rain; where are you already so late in the season?

The Kinneret lake is drying up as we all pray for rain. The eyes of an entire nation look to the sky and to the Kinneret.

I was up at 3:00 in the morning still struggling with jet lag. It was a wonderful feeling – just me and Jerusalem. It was foggy outside. Did this mean rain?

Finally, a normal winter morning in Jerusalem. Outside the distinct smell of fresh, wet air filled my nostrils. I smiled to myself on the way to the grocery to buy challah for Shabbat.

Everything was perfect, until I turned on the radio. Five top ranking air force personnel had been killed in a plane crash. More funerals. It's taken very hard.

The fog lifted. Another sunny day. Too bad.

It was announced that one thousand Ethiopian Jews would be arriving each month. And the Russians keep pouring in. It's a flood of immigrants. Thank God.

Now we need a flood of rain.

Housing Minister Sharon and Absorption Minister Peretz point fingers at each other as the immigrant log jam grows. Never have so many homes been promised to so many by two men with such huge egos."

"Balagan" (chaos).

In immigrant absorption centers throughout the land, new Israelis are lighting a menorah for the first time as they learn of the victories and miracles of old.

The Ethiopians were physically isolated from the Jewish world when the Chanukah events occurred. The Russians were robbed of the memory. Both were reborn this Chanukah.

Shabbat preparations are as lovely as usual. Flowers are sold on corners as a calm descends upon the city streets. Once again, the radio spoils it. An Arab factory worker stabbed three Jewish coworkers to death. Enraged Jewish protesters stoned Arab cars.

No one thinks of Saddam Hussein's threats when immediate danger lurks from fellow workers and neighbors.

I think, poor Israeli people. We need leadership that will stop it; leadership that knows what it wants and believes.

We deserve it.

Fifth candle:

The talk of the day is still the latest outrage in Jaffa. Four "Hamas" leaders are slated for deportation for inciting terror. The UN and the US are outraged. Israel is condemned. Israelis feel caught between Arab daggers and world hypocrite condemnation.

The country is moving to the "Right." It can be felt on the street as well in the polls.

Sixth candle:

If it weren't so tragic, it would be amusing; The so-called "pig law" divides Israelis lately. Some feel threatened and coerced by a law that tells them what to eat in restaurants. Others cannot conceive of pig sold in the holy land and in the holiest city of Jerusalem.

Only rockets aimed at them unite some Israelis. Never a dull moment.

Seventh candle:

I took my family for a Chanukah vacation to a hotel in Tiberias on the shores of the Kinneret (before it dries up).

I took the Coastal Road up instead of the Jordan Valley route because of "intifada" security precautions.

December sunshine; beautiful but very disappointing. We need rain.

I have never seen Tiberius so empty. No tourists. Hotels, restaurants – empty, pleasure boats – docked. A nation that dwells alone.

At the pool I noticed a number of men missing limbs. I realized that they were IDF veterans that paid the price for our security. There was certainly enough room for them at the hotel which has no tourists this season.

My children and I shared the pool with the vets. What does a child think and learn from this experience?

From the pool one gazes upon the magnificent Golan Heights across the lake. I wondered if perhaps some of these men's limbs were lost just there. I admired them as they made their way through the water with great determination. I hope my children notice.

Eighth candle:

Rain! Does this mean that we don't need to import water from Turkey?

Walking downtown in Jerusalem no one minded getting wet by the heaven-sent gift. No one rushed for cover or displayed discomfort. Smiles all around. Rain, rain don't go away!

Russia's Shevardnadze's resignation came as a shock. Was it good or bad for the Jews? The immediate fear was that the flow of Jews from Russia might be interrupted. Just then it was announced that a record-breaking number of Russians would be brought this week. Over one hundred per hour! Is this a last-minute scurrying before the door shuts again?

At the moment concerns about absorption problems give way to concern for immigration itself.

Will our people come home?

What a nation!

Another day of drama at the airport as Russian Jews stream into the country. They are a quiet, pensive bunch. It is understandable. Everything is new and unfamiliar. Uncertainty reigns. They come from a place where the government cannot be trusted. Not a simple step – even if it is to freedom and a dream.

I remember that these people had their Jewish identity squeezed from them by a monstrous dehumanizing society. Their return is a miracle of biblical, historic proportion.

A journalist asked one of them as he left the plane: "How is the situation in Russia?"

"Bad."

"What do you expect in Israel?"

"Good."

Empty hotels are being used temporarily to house the wave of newcomers. Where would they go if they were full of tourists as in normal years?

Every cloud has a silver lining.

And now the clouds were bringing us rain as well.

God, keep your eye on your people.

Happy Chanukah.

A Kippah In Jerusalem

When I was a teenager in Brooklyn, my passion was basketball. I was rather good and my goal was to become even better and prove myself on the court. Looking back, I understand that this was my way of gaining self-esteem because that is what I thought others appreciated. What else does a teenager want?

I was lucky to have a park across the street from where I lived, good old Ditmis park. Players came from all over the neighborhood to play on the popular courts with the best ball players in the area. I was able to just look out my window and see if there were guys in the park and join them. I spent lots of time on those courts.

As the neighborhood changed and Blacks moved in, new competition was felt. The language of the game changed as did the pace. It improved my game as I learned some things and made sure not to adopt others.

I remember that on the court it was not just basketball being played, but a meeting of cultures and even values. Suddenly, I felt that I represented the Jew who dared compete with Blacks in "their" game. It was not stated but there was a certain honor at stake on those courts. I felt I was representing not just myself. I wanted to earn their respect.

My third year in Brooklyn College (I did not play on their team because of Shabbat) I chose to study in Hebrew University for a year. Basketball fever had not yet left me.

In the gym, the Americans showed their stuff to the Israelis (for whom basketball was still a little-known American sport), and to each other. There was a tall Black American from Brandeis. I even remember his name. Unlike back in Ditmas Park where I eventually became one of the few Whites, here, he was a minority and I was the majority. It felt good.

Basketball can be very competitive and intimidation of the opponent can be both physical and verbal.

I recall as if it was yesterday how I forced myself to stand firm against a bigger and better player, not for myself, but hey, we were in a Jewish country. I thought if I was not intimidated by the same challenges in Brooklyn, I certainly wouldn't be here in my Jewish country. Was it only my imagination or was there an unstated point being vigorously being made on the court? I was proud that I took the bumps and was not intimidated.

When I completed my academic studies, I made Aliyah to Israel in 1977. I finally came home. Basketball was less a part of me by then.

I discovered that the same determination not to allow my Jewish identity and pride to be intimidated on the basketball court would be put to the test in other circumstances.

In 2000, the "second intifada" was launched by our "peace partners" of the Palestinian Authority. Horrible Arab violence dragged on for almost three years. Tourists disappeared and tour guides could not know when they would work again.

One day during that period, I visited the "Garden Tomb", where many Protestant Christians believe the crucifixion and burial was. I was acquainting myself with the site for a time when tourism might return. It is a very well kept series of gardens in the heart of East Jerusalem; a walled calm corner in the midst of the less calm Middle East surrounding it.

I remember well how the place was almost empty; no tourism. The pastor was very nice to me but he looked very concerned about something. I finally asked him what was worrying him.

He said, "I am not worried for myself. My staff and I are safe behind these walls. I see that you are wearing a kippah. Please do not take this the wrong way; do me a favor and don't walk these streets with your kippah on your head. It will draw 'their' attention and it could be very dangerous for you."

I was very embarrassed for the Jewish people in front of this man because he understood that our Jewish country cannot guarantee a Jew's security. A pastor had to warn me to be careful. I took that in for a moment. I thanked him for his concern and added, "how ironic this scene is. You, a pastor, are warning me, a Jew in the Jewish capital of the Jewish state, about hiding my identity as a Jew for my own safety. I must say, I am embarrassed." He was as well.

It is not Shalom Pollack who they want to intimidate. It is not about me personally. It is about the Jewish people. It is about the God of Israel. It is about Jewish pride – like on the courts.

I thought of those courts where I made similar decisions – to not be intimidated. I left the protection of the Christian walls to the streets of Jerusalem with my kippah on my head.

Nadia

I had the honor of sharing a bench with some of Israel's resolute soldiers for the Jewish People and the Land of Israel. I sat next to Prof. Auman, our latest Nobel laureate and Ms. Nadia Matar, founder of "Women in Green".

Former extreme left "Peace Now" leader, Mr. Mazuz, now the government attorney general, indicted her for insulting a public official.

It happened last summer in 2005 at the height of the mass expulsion of Jews from twenty-five flourishing communities and delivering those communities to the terrorists.

Mr. Yonatan Bassi volunteered to lead the civil and psychological war against the thousands of families about to be expelled. He was to sedate them through an arsenal of carrots and sticks, into leaving their homes willingly. He became one of the symbols of the expulsion.

Ms. Matar sent him a letter accusing him of playing a role in a way, worse than the Judenraat of the ghettos in Nazi occupied Europe. He wasn't ordered to choose his shameful job. He volunteered. Mr. Bassi wears a kippah and is thus identified with the orthodox in Israel. This was an important "qualification" mask for the psychological and public relations campaign to lull and fool the victims.

Nadia was cool and confident in the face of her accusers, certain of her path and of the future. Her lawyer, Mr. Sheftel made some interesting and revealing points:

Just a few days ago, another public servant, the Chief of Staff, General Chalutz, was the object of a "Peace Now" demonstration in front of his residence in which he was called a murderer – by Ms. Olmert, our prime minister's daughter! She has not been charged yet with insulting a public official.

A few years ago, a prominent cleric called for the death of a minister in the government. No charges, no arrests; there would definitely be widespread violent demonstrations.

Israel's first president, Mr. Chaim Weizman, and Israel's

first prime minister, Ben Gurion, were known to label Ze'ev Jabotinsky and Menachem Begin as Hitlerites and Fascists. Ben Gurion referred to Jabotinsky always as Vladmir Hitler.

So much for invoking certain words when criticizing a public official. The famous leftist artist Yigal Tomerkin was not arrested when he said that he understood the Nazis when he saw ultra-Orthodox Jews.

It was pathetic to see the young team of state prosecutors trying to babble some nonsense about the rule of law and civilized debate. Young upstarts trying to impress their bosses; sweating under their robes while they embarrassed themselves and their entire Jewish heritage in a Jewish courtroom.

Nadia, public enemy number one. May we be blessed with more Nadias.

On Eagles' Wings

I made Israel my home in 1977 after my first visit in 1971. No country in the world has undergone so much change and turbulence than this tiny one. Countries fifty times her size and population are hardly noticed by the world or its press. Israel has more front-page coverage than any country in the world except the USA – as of today.

The greening of the deserts, cutting edge technological breakthroughs, military prowess and the percentage of Nobel prize winners do not cease to amaze but it is not any of those that made me stop and marvel yesterday afternoon.

More than any of the wonders that is Israel, first and foremost, is that it is a Jewish country. This, more than anything else, is the exception to history. Never has a people returned to its home after two thousand years. We all know the rest – miracles beyond imagination have accompanied Israel from her inception.

Yesterday afternoon was one of those times when this miracle hit me afresh. There is a Russian immigrant living in my Jerusalem neighborhood. He has learned to read some of the prayers in Hebrew and seems to be making up for a lifetime robbed of Jewish identity in Communist Russia. He tries hard. He had nobody in the world except his very old mother and she had no one besides him until she passed away.

Yesterday I was one of the ten men he asked to come to the cemetery. He doesn't know ten men he can call upon. I guess because I made a point of greeting him in shul, he felt he could ask me and a few others.

I stood at the grave of this woman who had surely seen a lot in Russia. The Czar, Lenin, Stalin, Hitler – oh the joys of Mother Russia. She finally came home to rest in Jerusalem, the last stop for an old Jewess where her son collected a minyan for her. It probably never occurred to her that "Next year in Jerusalem" would actually happen and that the stones of Jerusalem would be her eternal companion.

Because the Russian immigrants are latecomers to the

Jerusalem cemetery, their plots are in a newer section – next to another group of recent returnees to the Land – the "Benai Menashe."

Where better to witness the miracle of the ingathering of the exiles than in a Jerusalem cemetery? As we helped the elderly immigrants with the reciting of the Psalms that were forbidden in Russia, Asian Jews were paying their respects a few feet away. They seemed like light years away, but this moment united the two most dissimilar groups one could imagine.

The Benai Menashe have a fascinating story. Their last home was in Manipur on the Burmese-Indian border. They have never forgotten their ancient roots after they were expelled from Israel over twenty-seven hundred years ago by Assyria.

I asked some of their younger people to read the inscription on the tombstone. It was in their own script which most of these, now Israelis, could hardly decipher. The deceased was one of the first to undergo official conversion and "rebirth" in 1975. His second rebirth occurred in 1988 when he came home to Israel. The younger generation are the new shoots springing up in the soil of Zion. The elder, now in that soil, lived to see it happen.

As the prophet said, "I will bring you from the corners of the earth on the wings of eagles." I saw them in a Jerusalem cemetery.

For me, this is what Israel is all about. This is the miracle of miracles.

In that cemetery, standing between two groups that have only one thing in common, I realized that my return from my part of the Jewish exile was far more than just personal choice. The same eagles that brought them, also brought me.

1 / 1992
Reserve Duty And A Secret

Army reserve duty, like taxes, is part of life in Israel. There were two yellow envelopes I did not welcome in my mailbox. One was from the tax man and the other a reserve duty notice.

Serving in the navy, I was a young reservist assigned to the coastal observation unit monitoring terrorist movements.

I made the trip from Jerusalem to Haifa, the navy's home base and from there I was sent to the northern tip of Israel near Lebanon. There were six of us from different walks of life. Reserve duty is the great equalizer. It is where the banker sleeps next to the street sweeper. It is a rather unique social experience.

In our group we had a lively young redheaded Russian immigrant. He spoke of his dream to open a pub in Tel Aviv in order to make enough money to buy a boat. He was going places for sure. A very nice guy and a good cook, which is a highly important skill in our tiny world.

There was an older fellow from the Caucasus Mountains of south Russia. He spoke very little Hebrew and even his Russian was poor I was told. What was he doing in the army? I felt sorry for him. He never took his days off. He preferred to stay and eat army food. I wondered why. I tried to communicate with him with no success.

The most memorable thing about my days off was coming home to my little children with my rifle and uniform. When I hugged them I understood better why I was serving.

Then there was the inevitable creep who you are stuck with for three weeks. He constantly smoked, turned the lights on and made noise when we were sleeping; had no regard for anyone but himself. It never ceases to amaze me. Was he so miserable in his own life? One learns a lot about people in the army.

We prepared our own food which was supplied daily from the home base. The arrival of our food reminded me of when I was a small boy in Brooklyn awaiting the grocery delivery and the goodies my mother ordered.

What we feared most were not terrorists slipping ashore, but a surprise inspection by our commander.

We were stationed on the top floor of an eight-story building owned by the "Jewish Agency." It housed elderly new immigrants from Romania and Russia. My knowledge of Yiddish allowed me a peek into some of their lives.

Desperate to escape from cramped quarters, I befriended an elderly Romanian lady. She prepared eggs and toast for me and I brought her tins of army food from which she was able to create something tasty. We enjoyed this arrangement and each other's company, but for some reason she wanted it to be our secret. Mysterious.

Her room had that old world feel. Her apron, tea cups, shoes. Everything felt like I imagined Romania of another time. What an unlikely combination; a Brooklyn boy in Israeli army uniform sipping tea with a Romanian bubby. When and where could this happen?

I have found that the most unlikely things can happen in Israel if you are open to them. During this round of duty, I was stationed atop a tall building in a closed glass cubicle (for when it was cold or rainy) looking far out at sea with various optical tools. My weapon was ready to repulse invaders. I actually had a big responsibility.

I witnessed the most beautiful sunset and sunrise from that booth. During raging storms, I observed the might of nature from within my little cubicle close to my beloved heater.

Each morning from my post I looked down on a group of Ethiopian children who had just arrived in Israel walking on the beach with their Israeli "counselor." As I waved to them, I felt as if I was waving to the prophets who foretold this entire miracle. In a few years I might be serving in the same army as these children. To which new immigrants might they themselves wave one day?

Well, the three weeks ended and we all returned to our families. Farewells were said and numbers were exchanged, never to be used, as usual. Uniforms and equipment were returned to the same bored faces who assigned them to us earlier and we were civilians again, until the next yellow envelope in my mailbox.

From Russia With Love

I live near the "Diplomat Hotel," now a government run residence for elderly Russian immigrants who never quite adapted to the new environment in Israel.

Whenever I see them waiting at the bus stop with their food trolleys and the inevitable extra piece of outerwear, I try to imagine their lives over there. They survived Stalin and Hitler to sit next to me at the Jerusalem bus stop.

They look about their new surroundings with a mixture of suspicion and perplexing study.

I think I know how they feel and so I try to break the ice with a smile and a "*boker tov*" greeting. With the first couple of tries I am either dismissed as an eccentric or a con man. What does this guy want from us? By the third try I sometimes make a friend. I realize that in the Communist paradise, trust of strangers and even family was not always safe. I know where it comes from, but I have this desire to make them feel at home – finally.

The other day, I connected with a nice elderly couple. Hebrew? *Nyet*. Yiddish? *Nu, a bisel* ... Some. It was rusty but he seemed to enjoy the opportunity to try it once again.

He must have wondered where my Yiddish came from. I explained that I was raised in the free Jewish state of Brooklyn.

We rode together on the bus and had a lively conversation using all six of our hands and various sounds.

They have one son, a brilliant mathematician who was studying and working at the university in Jerusalem.

So why were they not beaming? From the hand language and halting Yiddish, I understood that their son "grew his payot (side locks) long and prayed a lot." He is married and lives in Bnei Brak where he has a hard time making a living. Their only son forfeited his academic career to enter a life of unnecessary struggle. I totally understood.

We agreed on the difficulties and challenges that accompanied their son's choice but I was able to help them see the miracle in their son and families returning to Judaism, almost snuffed out by the Communists.

Torah, Mitzvot, Eretz Yisrael; a Jewish family...? As my grandfather would say in Yiddish, "*Ein klenekeit* – no small thing." They were somewhat comforted – I think.

As I got up from my seat and said goodbye, guess whose face stared at me? Good old Uncle Joe (Stalin!).

There was a Russian man who was proud to wear a T-shirt sporting Stalin's face. He is too young to remember the mass murderer, but for some reason he had a soft place in his heart for him.

What a coincidence. I had just spent time with two who survived his claws and here on a Jerusalem bus another Russian Jew displays him. I had to ask him why. Was it because he was so kind to the Jews?

He yelled at me in a very broken Hebrew, "You (and he pointed to my kippah) spread lies about everything and about Stalin too."

Why did he leave Mother Russia for a country full of fanatics and liars like me? Maybe it is the same reason thousands of Arabs will do anything to gain Israeli citizenship in a hated apartheid country called Israel.

Perhaps there is no contradiction between living in a country because it is a great place to live, yet hate it at the same time. It's a paradox that Israel tolerates.

The prophet Isaiah predicted, "There will be a time when good will be called evil and evil will be called good." I see the fulfillment of it daily on the streets of Jerusalem.

Return To My Roots

I was glad to come home to Israel after my two-week "roots pilgrimage." My family comes from "over there" in the "old country." In Belarus and the Baltic lands came one third of the Holocaust victims, including some of my family.

During the post-war Soviet occupation, there were no monuments erected to remember the Jewish victims of the Nazis and their local helpers. All monuments recorded only "Soviet" victims. When the Soviets conquered the areas from the Nazis, the local collaborators had hell to pay.

When the Russians left in 1990, the local authorities gave some attention to the Jews that "disappeared" from within their midst. This attention was not out of love for their former neighbors, but rather it was one of the steps taken to get closer to the West with their tourists, including Jewish visitors like me.

The locals hated the Russians and Communists much more than the Nazis. The Nazi period offered the locals great opportunity, including robbing and murdering Jews. Local Nazi collaborators are heroes today, with monuments and all. The hated Russians are gone. They would like to be allowed to celebrate the good old days without drawing too much attention from the West.

I felt in the shadows of two monsters, the Nazis and the Communists. Jews were the targets of both regimes. These lands were rarely a safe place for a Jew to live. Today very few Jews are left, but if you look hard enough, their ghosts of a thousand years are still there.

In my search for Jews, I visited synagogues where a pitiful handful of elderly men gather for a free meal and some company. Chabad was there, as always, to help.

I have nothing special to report about the current generation in these lands of the killing fields. They have their own problems. Corrupt inefficient government, external Russian threat, and an economy trying to find its way out of the rigid Soviet system and join the West.

Alcoholism and unemployment are high. Ethnic tensions with imported Russians simmer. Those who can, flee westward. I would not want to be in a bar amongst the locals and hear what they think about Jews. I would expect no surprises.

My guide in Minsk, Belarus, was a young man who made Aliyah to Israel, married a non-Jewish Russian and moved back to Belarus. He earns his living by taking people like me to Jewish sites. He learned Hebrew while in Israel but knows very little of Judaism. He is raising a non-Jewish family where the Jewish people were decimated.

In Vilna, my guide was a local Jewish woman who also lived in Israel for a while and then returned to Lithuania. She really knew her stuff, both Jewish and non-Jewish history. She says she loves living in Vilna and is involved in local politics. I noticed that she picked up trash from her beloved streets.

I asked her, "Is there anything that you don't like about Vilna?" She thought for a moment and said, "I know that if the Nazis returned, many of my neighbors would happily cooperate with them again."

Many thoughts entered my mind. One was, "You call this your beloved home?" I wanted to say, "You can always come home. You don't have to live with a nightmare."

I kept the thoughts to myself. Who am I to judge? I was just happy that I was going home soon.

Unforgivable

Mazal tov! In shul this morning a Bar Mitzvah boy was called up to the Torah; his adoring family and friends cheering him on.

Not members of our shul, I assume they needed a place for the simcha. The celebrant had new shoes; high top basketball sneakers. His father wore shorts and a rainbow color shirt. Precariously perched on their heads were the kind of white silky kippahs available to guests in some shuls. The grandparents had their own kippahs and were more conservatively dressed.

The young man struggled mightily with the reading which I assume he had well practiced. The blessing on the Torah was an ordeal for him as well. Same for his father.

I watched the grandfathers. They looked like fans watching their favorite team struggle to remain on the field. The father and son did not have a clue. The shul experience was clearly not one they were used to. For these Israeli Jews, it all seemed so strange. This is no accident. It is a choice. At least they chose to commemorate and celebrate the Bar Mitzvah.

I have a cousin who lives on a well-established Leftist kibbutz who never "gave" his son a Bar Mitzvah. This is a common ideological choice of the secular anti-religious elite.

The family in my shul this morning was not motivated by Left ideology. They represent many Israeli Jews today. The grandfathers were probably born in Arab lands and have unbroken generations of Torah observance behind them. They however, chose not to make an effort to pass the Torah link to their children. They were complacent that their values would somehow be their children's, just as their parents' values were theirs. They did not fulfill the commandment – "And you shall teach your children."

Why the shift?

One can say that the immigrant experience is always challenging, and exhausting. Things happen. Energies are reallocated. New ways are adopted as old ones fade.

"Success" in the new country is paramount. Prices are paid. This is common amongst immigrants. American Jewry and its loss of identity is the classic example. But this is Israel. They returned home to a Jewish land to practice Judaism as free Jews, as opposed to the hostile one that they fled.

The choice in Israel was not Judaism or survival. Perhaps it was Torah or success?

The great tragedy of the Jews that fled Arab lands to Israel was on display in my shul this morning. In the case of the Jews from Arab lands, their cultural, religious and spiritual demise was largely engineered.

Engineered by whom? By my cousin and his fellow anti-religious Ashkenazi elites who see themselves as the nobility of the "new Israel" and know what's best.

It was necessary for the "primitive masses" from the Arab lands to become "Israeli" as fast as possible. For their "own good" the establishment controlled every practical need of these immigrants, offering material rewards and opportunities for their souls.

The "red pass" of the ruling Socialist (Mapai) party was the key. How does one get that red pass? By either joining and voting for the right party or by "doing things their way."

What was their way? It started with sending your children to the "right" schools; the kind that makes sure a Jewish child is a stranger in a shul. ... A tree is only as strong as its roots.

I heard a great rabbi say, "Of all the crimes of the Left, uprooting Torah from the Sephardic Jews is clearly an unforgivable one."

The Shalva Heroes

"The Shalva Band, a group of musicians with disabilities, will pull out of the race to represent Israel at the Eurovision because of the group's Shabbat observance. The Jerusalem Post confirmed Tuesday that the band has informed Keshet, the network that airs Hakochav Haba (Rising Star), that it could not continue in the competition."

The above item should make every Jew very proud of these idealistic youngsters. One can only imagine how hard this group of artists worked to overcome their personal disabilities and get a shot at what is every aspiring artist's dream: The Eurovision!

Their choice: Fame and glory and the reward of years of toil and dreams. The other – principles and a dream that traverses time.

They chose that elusive thing called eternity over what is referred to today as "realizing one's full potential." For them, their choice was their full potential.

Fast forward a few decades and imagine these young idealists having a talk with their grandchildren. They will tell them how once upon a time, they had to make a very difficult choice; personal glory (ego?) or the values of their own grandfathers and grandchildren; of their people: Shabbat or me?

Back in the thirties, Chaim Nachman Bialik, the great Israeli writer, coined the phrase, "more than the Jews kept the Sabbath, the Sabbath kept the Jews." He himself perhaps did not observe but understood its role in preserving the Jewish people. The holy Shabbat has always been the single major alliance between the Jewish nation and their God.

When Jews fled Europe to the security and freedom of the USA, they faced challenges shared by the other new arrivals. The Jews, however, faced added dilemmas and challenges; greatest of all was Shabbat. Some threw their prayer books overboard as soon as the Statue of Liberty came into sight. They could not wait to jettison it all in order to be an "American." For those it was not a dilemma. It's not to those that I refer.

I am speaking of the many who did want to continue being loyal Jews and raise Jewish families even in America. Who can judge them? The six-day work week includes Saturday. What to do?

During the depression years, things got really tough. Yet, there were those who made huge efforts to put bread on the table and also keep the holy Shabbat. Often, they would attend a very early service on Shabbat morning and then go to work. In the beginning, it was with a heavy heart. But eventually, one gets used to things and to change, especially if others are doing the same. How many of their grandchildren are Jewish?

Many Jews strove mightily to find employment that was Shabbat-friendly. They pushed carts or opened small businesses and later became professionals. Both my grandfathers passed this difficult test. It was heroic. I have stories that I tell my grandchildren. It is about fortitude and principle that will be heard.

The Shalva band is what the Jewish people are all about; what we have always been about. In Israel, not everyone sees the Shalva band as heroes. They missed an opportunity at what life is all about – success and fame. Fools! Fanatics!

There are those in Israel for whom their identity as a Jew is unclear at best. For some, it is a burden.

In 1996, when Shimon Peres surprisingly lost the election to Netanyahu, he was asked by a journalist: "Who lost?"

He answered, "The Israelis."

Then, "Who won?" he was asked.

He said, "The Jews."

The Shalva Jews won. The Jewish state should be very proud. Israel should be proud.

1 / 1999

My Reservist Journal

Entry 1 – The first day was typical – hurry up and wait. Why do I always rush to report on time? I never learn.

So, we are finally moved in. Our base is a converted house on the main street in downtown Daharia, an Arab town almost an hour south of Hebron. Our "villa" is home to forty young conscripts (artillery brigade) and us, eight "older" reservists.

We are the responsible and mature drivers of the patrol jeeps with the younger men as our passengers. I've learned to take orders from men half my age and to respect them very much. Out of uniform they are just kids, but they know their jobs and do them very well. I was impressed.

Fortunately, six of my reservist comrades were very nice and easy to live with. Unfortunately, there was that inevitable sour soul that seemed to be sent just to disturb. At least he did not smoke.

Entry 2 – My first patrol. I was introduced to my jeep. No mirror, horn or parking brake. We were warned not to exceed 30 kilometers per hour and not trust our brakes or any indicators. We weren't the IDF's priority.

Down the road from our villa is the very filthy market of Daharia. With nightfall the market is still. After 9:00 pm the only movement there is of wild dogs and large rats.

Five minutes into my first patrol we were ambushed by a rock attack. My arm was hit. The young soldiers sprinted from the jeep in pursuit. They told me to stay with the vehicle with my blue roof lights on to "show a presence."

I asked myself, did I really want to show a presence and be a target to those lurking in the darkness? But orders are orders. I was alone in my jeep; motor running, blue lights announcing that the IDF is here!

I fingered my rifle and thought here I am, my first night and I might just have to shoot someone or be badly hurt, or worse. What goes through one's mind?

The soldiers returned after what seemed like an eternity, disappointed because the attackers got away. I was thankful that the rock did not hit my face.

What is a nice Jewish boy from Brooklyn doing in a place like this?

There are a number of Russian immigrants amongst the young conscripts. They were on fire. Great soldiers. I was gratified to see how these young men adopted their new country with zeal.

Every once in a while I drove my patrol jeep to the regional base where we refueled. On one occasion, I saw a very curious thing. Late one evening, an Arab vehicle drove up, and someone deposited a body at the gate and then sped off. I wasn't sure if the person was dead or wounded. The soldiers at the base were not particularly alarmed. I later learned that in the southern Hebron area there were ongoing blood feuds between clans and that they would deliver the dead and wounded at the gate of the Israeli base for continued care.

What a bizarre situation. They maim and kill each other and leave the results at the door of the Israelis. What does this reflect? What do they expect us to do now? Are we the symbol of responsibility that they are incapable of accepting? Was it similar to children fighting and then turning to their parents to lick the wounds and arbitrate calm? It was as confusing as it was shocking.

Entry 3 – Holocaust Memorial Day. The 10:00 a.m. siren called us to attention in honor of the day. Zvika, with "ants in his pants," stood next to me for that moment. He was always helpful and playful. When the sirens fell silent, he turned to me and for the first time I saw a serious look on his face. He said, "I am so proud to wear this uniform. There WILL not be another Holocaust." That was the last time I saw Zvika in a serious mood. I was proud, too.

Daharia is a microcosm of the general "situation." What is to be done with the "territories?"

I compared the problem to a person holding a snake at arm's length to prevent it from biting. How long can one function by holding on to a snake? Israelis do not want to rub shoulders with an Arab population. The Arabs of Israel are enough of a challenge. However, there is every indication that if we release the snake, it will go for our necks in a flash. What to do?

This was just a couple of years after the "Oslo" solution and it was not working out very well.

I fear for and greatly admire the Jewish communities in this area where so many snakes lurk. What will be with these Jewish communities if the army leaves the area? I shuddered to think.

The soldiers came from every background and political persuasion. They shared a common dim view of the Arabs we were securing. They were frustrated by the constant cat and mouse game in which Arab taunts and challenges could not be met with the force that the soldiers would prefer. There are very strict rules and the Arabs know how to take advantage.

Some of the young soldiers react by acting in an overbearing, at times even mean way. Put a gun into the hands of some of these young men and they act like children playing soldier. But they know the rules. I would hate to see our people at the mercy of Arab young men playing soldiers with rifles. It would look very different.

One of our tasks was to check Arabs for valid entry and working papers. Work in Israel is a privilege for which thousands wait in line from before sunrise. They can make five times what their people in the corrupt Palestinian Authority will offer.

One man, searching for a sympathetic face, found mine. He said, "why do you make us wait so long in the sun? I am a father of eighteen children. We are not all terrorists."

I felt for him but thought to myself, yes, you are not all terrorists, but all of our children are targets of terrorists. Your eighteen children are safe. So, wait.

Dilemma.

Entry 4 – A beautiful Shabbat morning. I had the honor of reciting the kiddush for the entire group. I was the local "rabbi" I guess. Most of the nonobservant enjoyed the moment of spirit, as army rations became a Shabbat meal – a break from the rest of the week. It tasted special.

Speaking of a break, a soldier's most important time was soon to be mine – leave. Three days away from the villa and Daharia.

As I reached Jerusalem far from the military drudgery, I felt even more like a soldier. I walked amongst the people I was protecting, the ones who would not throw boulders at me, but appreciate my uniform and gun. That feeling grew as I reached home and then embraced my children. I could not help but ask myself which of those Arabs in Daharia waiting at the military barrier hoped to reach my children and not a day's work.

Would my children need to be soldiers in the future?

Entry 5 – I sit on the porch of the villa saying my morning prayers, wrapped in tallit and tefillin facing north towards Jerusalem. Below, Arabs walk by and look up at the strange site. They don't know exactly what to make of it, but I believe they knew it was about prayer. They don't look twice.

The Israeli flag flaps overhead as across the road a PLO flag does the same above a school. I feel we are in a historical twilight zone; not clear at all. I felt that my colleagues and I were the last players on this chessboard. Things were changing. For the better?

I cannot feel hostile towards random individual Arabs. I cannot grimace at strangers in the street.

From my position on the veranda, I meet the eyes of passersby. I smile and they look back at me with incredulity and hurry on. When they tell their friend about what just happened and they look to verify, I wipe the smile off my face. It's my little game of sowing confusion amongst the enemy. Who said reserve duty is not creative?

Wouldn't it be nice if we could all smile at each other? I was taught to do that. I know that their education is very different.

Golda Meir once said, "if Arab mothers loved their children more than they hated ours, there would be peace."

Entry 6 – Reserve duty ends as it began; hurry up and wait. It was really quite beautiful and touching how a small group of strangers forms a bond in a short time.

We sincerely promised to stay in touch, which we did not of course, but something special remained.

My Son And Honenu

I learned of "Honenu" in the summer of 2005 when my teenage son joined thousands of idealistic youth in the protests against the mass expulsion of Jews from their homes in Gush Katif and Shomron.

The government suspended (unofficially) the rule of law to guarantee that the "Disengagement" went smoothly. The media, legal system, law enforcement – the entire bureaucracy – was mobilized to get the dirty job done smoothly. Still, wonderful youth, like my son, "went south" to stand with the Jewish families facing forced expulsion from their homes.

The police used every illegal trick and brutality to discourage this exhibition of Jewish pride and determination. Sweeping brutal arrests were made with no legal basis. It didn't matter. The cops knew they had the backs and blessings of their bosses – all the way to the very top.

My son constantly witnessed brutality. They were herded into a large outdoor holding area under the merciless sun, without knowledge of what their crime was, or when they would be released. At one point he risked being beaten by a cop when he intervened as the cop was beating an elderly man. He remembers a lone man carrying a briefcase approaching the compound and having a talk with the commander. After he left, the entire group was released with no explanation as to why they were arrested in the first place.

It turns out that this man was a lawyer from Honenu that came to the rescue of my son and the many other abused youth. Honenu provides legal aid to Jews who find themselves alone against the kind of system that abused my son.

Many of the secular Left perceive the idealistic community as a deeper threat than rockets coming over from Gaza. One can always build walls and shelters and hide until the terrorists decide it's enough.

Rockets may kill some Jews but these strange youths represent something much more dangerous to them – a challenge to their leadership and moral legitimacy, a challenge that must be quashed in its infancy.

A group of yeshiva students had just left the Temple Mount after prayers on Jerusalem Day. They were suddenly accosted by knife and club wielding Arabs lying in ambush in the narrow lanes of the Old City. Suffering head and other injuries, the Jewish students were relieved when the Israeli police arrived.

Alas, as happens all too often, the police roughly arrested the Jewish youth. What were these strange looking "right wing fanatics" doing in "Arab" territory? Probably looking for trouble again. No Arabs were arrested.

The police refused to share the security camera footage with the court when challenged by Honenu attorney David Halevi. After a harrowing experience, first at the hands of an Arab mob and then by the Israeli police, they were finally released, bruised in body and spirit.

What must these patriotic, God-fearing youth think of their own police and leaders?

A few days later it happened yet again. In the Jewish pioneering village of Yitzhar in the Shomron, police barged in on sleeping youths in the middle of the night and dragged them out of bed. They were accused of torching Arab vehicles.

Five youths, most under the age of eighteen, were thrown in jail and then brought before a judge.

A "Honenu" attorney was rushed to the scene and the "nationalist youth" were released after the police could produce no evidence against the "usual suspects."

It happens all the time. The youth are bewildered. Who is the enemy? Who is supposed to protect them?

These youth – lovers of their land and their people are weird – a clear danger to the system and – most importantly to their claim to leadership.

As Adi Kedar, the Honenu attorney explained: "Apparently even with minors – girls, boys – they often try to make cases by bringing them to harsh interrogation facilities if they think it will break them. Conditions range from tying them to chairs, making the room exceedingly hot or cold, blinding lights; in some cases, torture.

Break them? Break what exactly? Regardless of age or sex,

illegal and brutal methods are used to break these youth and "mainstream" them. Their devotion to our land and ideals is threatening to those who have long forgotten what that means.

They are never totally alone as long as Honenu is here to defend them, as I learned from my son in 2005.

Hadassah

The "Hadassah Women" were coming to town. This called for many buses, drivers and guides. A travel company called upon me to be one of the guides. As usual, I was glad for the work. Self-employed tour guides and especially those limited due to Shabbat observance grab any job offered.

I was happy to guide Jewish women active on behalf of Israel.

This should be interesting and hopefully I can share my own passion and knowledge for our land with these caring ladies.

It was 1995, two years after the Oslo treaty with Yasser Arafat's PLO. "Land for peace" was the rage. If you did not cheer the "peace," you were not part of the "forces of light." My kippah marked me as from "the dark side."

Our first morning out, I took the microphone and began guiding. As the bus drove down the Bar Ilan Road, a major street in Jerusalem, we passed a historical point. There is no official marker of its significance and most don't realize what is here. I knew that I should share it with the Hadassah ladies who came from so far away to learn about our beloved country.

The "green line" where pre-1967 Jerusalem (Israel) ends and post-1967 begins, runs invisibly across the road. On both sides of the line are Israeli neighborhoods. Who would know that this was once a hostile border?

I thought it would be interesting and important to give my guests a geographic perspective on the layout of Jerusalem and understand what the oft repeated political term "green line" means.

There was silence and perplexed looks throughout the bus when I pointed it out and explained its significance. I was not surprised. I understood that this information challenged long held assumptions.

In those days of Oslo celebrations, the term "green line" and post-1967 territories indicated where the anti-peace "settlers" lived, out there in the "occupied territories" surrounded by indigenous Arabs who just wanted peace. Those "areas" were controversial and stood in the way of peace.

They did not imagine that the Arab demand for a return to the "green line" for peace included the schools and supermarkets they were looking at.

Did Arafat demand this too and not just areas "out there" that no one wants anyway? Who knew? They never gave it a thought, until that moment when I pointed it out to them.

The silence was broken when a woman stormed to the front of the bus and grabbed the microphone from my hand. She adamantly made it clear that "Hadassah supports the 'peace process' and the Rabin government!"

When she finished, I calmly told her, "I simply pointed out a historical / geographical fact. I did not speak for or against any government."

I understood her hysterical outburst. I had the audacity to take the blinders off the docile sheep she was herding.

Hadassah was part of the "forces of light." Facts weren't going to change that.

That very day I was called into the office of the tour company that hired me. I was told, "Shalom, I know these ladies can be difficult at times, but I must ask you not to return to work. I hope you understand."

I did.

Maccabees, Where Are You?

*W*e come not to these lands as a foreign conqueror. Our *forefathers were forcefully expelled from our God-given lands by the Babylonians and by His grace, we are back in our homeland. We are returning to what is rightfully ours. You are sitting on our lands and the time has come for you to remove yourselves from them.*

This clear and unapologetic statement was made by Yochanan Horkinus, the Maccabee leader 2,100 years ago.

After his father and uncles (the five Maccabee brothers) won a prolonged war of liberation and religious liberty from the Greek world power, Yochanan turned his attention to the foreign occupiers that filled the vacuum during Jewish exile and military impotence.

It was time to reassert Jewish sovereignty in all the land of Israel. That meant all those peoples who had trespassed while the Jews were in exile had to leave. The process of reconquest led to the establishment of the widest borders since the time of King David and Solomon.

Fast forward two thousand years.

The Jewish people miraculously return from, not seventy years of exile, but close to two thousand, after the worst blow ever delivered to any people.

Despite impossible odds, the tattered remains of the Jewish people rebuilt themselves and reclaimed their homeland; the same one that Yochanan the Maccabee did twenty-one hundred years ago.

The latest liberation came in stages and at a heavy price – just as it was in the times of the Maccabees.

However, unlike the Maccabees, the leaders of the modern returnees did not understand that it was God who had guided us with extraordinary miracles.

They would never make a speech such as Yochanan the Maccabee did when returning to the land.

In 1948 and 1967, open miracles put us on the way to liberating our lands, as in the time of the Maccabees. Then came the Oslo Accords.

Instead of claiming and securing sovereignty over lands liberated in the miraculous Six-Day War of 1967, our "leaders" invited enemies who claimed OUR land as their own. We armed them so that they would PROTECT us! This "protection" cost thousands of Jewish lives, so far.

The entire saga returned to me yesterday when I attended a tour of the magnificent excavated Maccabean palaces in Jericho. I visited this unique (there are no other Maccabean remains found in Israel) site years ago, before the dangers and restrictions that came with the Oslo "peace." I was wowed by the enormity of the find and felt directly attached to the Maccabees at that moment.

The palaces, swimming pools, the mikvah, and especially the synagogue were spectacular. It was an impressive excavation that stood by itself with no buildings or agriculture anywhere near it. It stood alone in its brilliance as a rare gem should.

I have not been back there for many years. The Oslo peace, you know.

Yesterday, Chanukah, I returned. The excavations are in "area C." This, according to the Oslo agreement, is an area under full Israeli control, as opposed to A and B in which big red signs warn Jews not to enter due to potential physical harm. It's the peace you know. No Jews allowed. (Is this what they mean by Israeli apartheid?)

A number of groups have pleaded with the military administration in charge of the "territories" to allow Jews to visit the spectacular site – at least once a year, on Chanukah.

Finally, permission was granted for one day out of the entire year. That is how I found myself attending a tour of the site that I visited with such ease years ago. Now there was a very large military presence that protected us from the locals. I suppose the force was also there to make sure that Jews did not wander off into "their" territory, which would have been a major political issue or perhaps end in a lynching.

The site is almost unrecognizable. The Arabs use the surrounding areas as garbage dumps. Where I saw, years ago, open spaces around the site, now are cluttered with an assortment of huts, animal pens, hothouses, and garbage. Arabs continually damage the priceless artifacts. The Israel authorities do nothing to stop it.

This criminal negligence is common all over the "territories." However, when it comes to enforcing the law against Jews in the "areas," there is never a lack of resources or determination. Rule of law is paramount.

Needless to say, my Chanukah visit to the Maccabee palace made me think of my visits there so many years ago; the pre-Oslo visits that filled me with pride and joy made it very clear then why I left the USA and came home.

The wonderful speech of Yochanan was the exact opposite of the warning on the big red signs enforcing apartheid in Israel that forbid Jews to enter parts of our beloved land.

Yesterday, I and many others on the tour were perplexed. We wistfully asked each other where are the Maccabees today?

Will they return, before it's too late?

Jewish Generals

Former IDF Chief of Staff and Defense Minister Shaul Mofaz gave a Memorial Day speech at Tel Aviv University on Tuesday.

"We will use any means to ensure that the Israeli society is based on equality, ethics and justice," he said. "We must not lose our morals or our purity of arms, even during the most difficult times. No small number of soldiers and commanders have endangered their own lives, and even injured or killed for the sake of these values. This shows the legitimacy of our path."

This is the same Mofaz, when chief of staff, watched as IDF soldier Madhat Yusuf bled to death defending Joseph's Tomb in Shechem from the assaults of "Palestinian security personnel" in October 2000.

Rather than risk confrontation with our "peace partners," Mofaz, on the scene, observed delirious Arab mobs assail and desecrate our holy site and shoot at our soldiers cowering inside.

Incredibly, he put his faith in his "Palestinian" counterpart, terrorist Gabril Rajub, who assured him that the attacks would stop and an ambulance was on the way. The ambulance never arrived. Our soldier bled to death – but the "peace process" lives.

We see a twisted non-Jewish mindset. For example, our current deputy chief of staff, Yair Golan, sees "a parallel between Israel today and Nazi Germany of the 1930s." Former prime minister and chief of staff Ehud Barak said that if he were a Palestinian, he would "take up arms against us" too. He understands them. Chief of Staff Benny Ganz added his voice to the gospel that our soldiers' lives should be sacrificed to save "innocent enemy civilians." Of course, these self-appointed keepers of morality happily hand our land to armed enemies at every opportunity, even, or especially, if accompanied with mass expulsion of our people from their homes. "Morality" can come at a high price.

This Memorial Day we remember the 24,447 soldiers who gave their lives for us, plus thousands more killed by Arab terror. Add to that, tens of thousands crippled in body or mind or their families who will never be the same.

Perhaps we can now better understand why Israel has not won a war since 1973. (We have fought five since then; three in Gaza against Hamas and two in Lebanon following our retreat from those areas, for peace and morality.)

The powerful Jewish army is shackled by men who don't have a clue about what a Jewish value is.

Our terror enemies that surround us (after we allow them to flourish and grow) determine the right time for the next "round." They are not deterred by the "very moral" IDF.

Dan Halutz was the chief of staff during the second Lebanon war in 2006. Before sending men into (disastrous) battle totally unprepared, he made sure to take the time to sell his entire stock portfolio. Stocks and war don't go well together. He was thinking of his stocks as he sent Jewish soldiers to be killed. ... Another expert on "true Jewish values."

Exactly one year before that debacle, Halutz presided over the well-planned and executed campaign in Gaza – the one in which he expelled ten thousand Jews from their homes and handed it to Hamas. He is very proud of that highly moral achievement.

Who said our moral generals are not efficient and successful when it really counts?

On this Memorial Day we remember our beloved fallen and pray for Jewish leaders.

Jewish.

Will We Be Ready Next Time?

Happy Jerusalem Day! In June 1967, the Jewish People realized a dream that was in our hearts from the moment we were expelled from our beloved holy city and Temple by the Romans two thousand years ago.

Jerusalem has never for one moment left the thoughts and prayers of Jews in every corner of the far-flung and bitter exiles. We are living their dream come true!

We celebrate the once in a history honor to live a dream of two thousand years. The spirit of those who kept the dream alive assured that there are still a Jewish People today. We are obliged to thank them for enduring throughout.

Why are we the chosen generation? I don't think we are better than our forefathers. Perhaps God has a time table that follows His logic. Do we appreciate it?

When our Temple Mount was liberated, the excited soldiers flew a homemade flag over the golden dome that sat on our holiest site. The shocked Muslim authorities handed the keys to our brave men and our holiest of mounts was ours again.

The flag flew proudly – for four hours. Then, Defense Minister Moshe Dayan ordered it to be taken down.

Why? He said it was unwise to humiliate the defeated Arabs. I suppose he believed they would respond in a positive manner, such as not denying that we ever had a Temple at all.

He and many of his generation of the elite ruling class took arrogant pride in denying God and His role in history. They were the new super Sabra generation that replaced God. Sensitivity to those who would kill us was their wisdom that no God could comprehend.

In Hebron, Dayan also ordered the flag (that chief IDF rabbi, Rabbi Goren, proudly hoisted atop the building) down from the Tomb of the Patriarchs, a place that the Muslims turned into a mosque and humiliatingly banned Jews for the last thousand years. Dayan was confident he knew how to turn enemies into friends.

The awestruck Arabs who just the day before were calling for Jewish blood wanted only to flee for their lives! Had they indeed fled there would be no Arabs in our land who want to murder us; no "Palestinian" Terror Authority. No Hamas. No security walls. No tunnels. No intifada. No living in fear.

But Dayan knew better. He actually prevented them from fleeing over the Jordan River and sent them right back into our heartland. He was sure that would win their hearts and applause all over the world.

God did His best. Even miracles must be acted upon. The best car in the world must have someone willing to turn the ignition key.

I try to imagine the collective joy and amazement of generations of dreamers as their spirits accompany our soldiers fighting through the lanes of Jerusalem. They reach the place of their dreams and then ... Moshe Dayan and his self-congratulating blasphemous illusions take over. History could have been different.

We were taken off guard by the miracle of 1967 and we did not have a leadership that responded with the humble gratitude expected.

Will we be ready to respond differently when God grants us a second chance?

Corona And Yom Kippur

This was the first Yom Kippur in the era of Coronavirus. Each year I notice how the shul I attend draws Israelis at the opening and ending of the day; at Kol Nidre and Neila. Not "in their natural element," they peep into windows, loiter outside, wearing what they deem appropriate for the annual occasion; they are pulled to the moment.

What is the attraction? Each year I look at the faces of those drawn to the shul with what seems like an urgency not to miss the fleeting moments. I wonder what it means?

Many of our People seem to be clinging to the last strands that connect them to the "old time religion." Are they covering their "theological bets?"

Maybe they wonder, perhaps there is something to this day of forgiveness after all? Perhaps it is a need for solidarity with other Jews and our tradition at least once a year?

This year all the shuls were locked, which brought the once a year happening to the streets.

The Arnona neighborhood where I have lived for the last fifteen years was totally secular not long before I arrived. The rabbi of the main shul in which I pray (now there are many others) told me that thirty years ago it was difficult to gather a minyan (a ten-man quorum) in the neighborhood.

Today, a good number of the residents are observant. Many are North American and Europeans who brought the "old religion" to the secular Israeli neighborhood. In the streets this year, the many minyanim in the various shuls contributed to the unique sounds and sights of the special day. Ashkanazi, Sephardi, Chabad; Jews of every stripe contributed to the Jewish rainbow on the streets.

The "*pintele Yid*" who attends shul once a year in Israel is different from his counterpart in the Diaspora. Outside Israel, streets are not closed on Yom Kippur. It is not a national holiday. Commerce and government do not shut down. The media do not shut down. The public arena remains unchanged. The language of prayer is a strange sound. The *"pintele"* spark in the heart of Diaspora Jews must overcome a multitude of obstacles and distractions for it to be ignited and burn even for a fleeting moment.

I imagine that this year, the once-a-year Jews living as a minority may have stayed home and did not dare fill their busy streets as one does freely in Jerusalem.

This unusual Yom Kippur on the streets of my Jerusalem neighborhood gave me food for thought. Thanks to Corona on Yom Kippur, I understood yet again why I chose to come home.

Ethiopians And Druze

What do Ethiopian Jews and the Israeli Druze community have in common? Both are unique groups, citizens of Israel with a strong sense of identity.

A few years ago, I was in the Jewish Agency in Jerusalem where they were preparing a display of the dramatic rescue of Ethiopian Jewry and their return to Zion.

From time immemorial, the Jews of Ethiopia like Jews the world over, longed for "next year in Jerusalem!" They walked for weeks in the deserts. Not all made it, as wild animals, slave traders and the elements took their toll. This was a modern Exodus story. Is there anything more dramatic or inspiring?

A particular poster caught my eye. It captured the moment a young Ethiopian mother with her baby on her back took their first steps in the Promised Land. With her traditional colored, modest clothing and the wonder in her eyes, it was an iconic picture.

Next to that moving scene was a poster depicting another young Ethiopian woman. This one displayed what successful integration into Israel looks like. Gone was the simple, modest clothing replaced by tight-fitting jeans and top. She looked Israeli, which means she could be anything now, maybe even a Jew.

The two posters were a few feet from each other but a world apart – Was this the dream of Ethiopian Jewry?

When I shared my thoughts with a young employee of the Agency, she did not understand my observation. Indeed, this was exactly the success that was hoped for. Ethiopian Jews had made it. Finally, they are "Israelis." They are modern and liberated. How far away was this from what her parents had hoped for her? She would now be identified as a young Black woman wherever she may go. In Ethiopia, she was identified as Jewish. That was lost. The Israeli Agency worker did not begin to understand what I was saying.

I had occasion to witness the yearly mass gathering of the

Ethiopian community as they celebrated the ancient holiday that remembered Jerusalem. In Ethiopia, they would gather once a year on a hill and face Jerusalem with prayer and praise, longing for the day as did Moses on Mount Moab where he longed for, but could not enter the Land.

Today in Jerusalem they gather in their tens of thousands, this time overlooking the Temple Mount. How wonderful to see our brothers home with us, fulfilling their dream! Hundreds of elders and rabbis (called kayses) in their traditional festive best is a joy to see. Thousands of their flock gathered, facing the Temple Mount.

Unfortunately, large parts of the flock have wandered from the path and are floundering in dangerous fields.

I saw these lost sheep. The bus I was riding in was targeted as we drove by. Threatening looks and less than friendly words yelled at us by throngs of bored teenagers strolling slowly across the street showing who owned the road.

Was I in Jerusalem or in a no-go neighborhood in Brooklyn? They looked and dressed like them. They crossed the street like them, as I recall.

Was it supposed to be this way? Were they saved from the long Exile for this? The young Jewish Agency lady probably sees this as the "price of progress."

I saw other young Ethiopians that day. Calm, disciplined, dressed in a respectable fashion, part of a Benai Akiva youth group. Some were group leaders engaged in organizing constructive activities appropriate for the occasion. Their faces radiated purpose and respect for others and for themselves. What a difference. I wonder if there is a Jewish Agency poster of them?

The grave mistakes being made with so many Ethiopian youth have been made with Jewish immigrants expelled from Arab lands that arrived in Israel in the fifties. Yes, a new Jew was then also created by a non-Torah Israel.

The "Black Panthers" protest riots and total alienation were the result. I imagine there were Jewish Agency posters then, too.

The common denominator to the above is one word – Identity. Do we appreciate who we are and why we returned to this land?

Many of our problems, both internal and external, can be linked to that one word – Identity. Who we are, why we returned to this special land and what obliges us is the key.

Which brings me to the Druze. The Druze community comprises about 2% of Israel's population. They are Arabs but have their own "secret religion." A simple, rural people, they can be fierce fighters when they must. They are loyal to the powers that be as long as they are treated fairly and if the government is perceived to be in control with clear direction.

During Israel's War of Independence, the Druze, like everyone else, believed the Jewish state had no chance and so they fought against the Jews on the side of the Arabs. When it became clear that the Jews were going to win, they switched and ended up on the winning side. The Druze like a winner. They have a healthy sense of where the winds are blowing – a necessity for survival in the region.

After the war, their elders urged Israel to take their sons into the IDF thus ensuring a pact between them and the winners. Indeed, the Druze community has always been an example of cooperation and respect between the Jewish state and its minorities.

This was true as long as they felt their patron was a winner. Since Oslo and subsequent retreats, the abandonment of our South Lebanon allies and Arab terror onslaughts, the Druze have been having second thoughts. They are Israel's litmus test. If they are loyal and respectful of the Jewish state, then we know we are ok. Keep your eye on the Druze.

Last month there was a pogrom in Pek'in, a Galilee village with a Druze majority and a few Jewish families. The excuse for the riot was a cell phone antenna. The result was all the Jewish homes were torched or ransacked. A Jewish policewoman was abducted and ransomed for arrested Druze rioters.

Are the Druze smelling the changing winds? The list of increasing Druze challenges to Israeli authority is well known and worrisome.

This would not happen in the pre-Oslo (1993) days, when Jews had a stronger identity. They see how Israel falls over itself to ape all things non-Jewish and how she appeases our neighbors, including giving them our land.

The Druze do not understand this behavior, but sense that something is not kosher with their erstwhile patrons and model. The Druze like a winner.

So, what do Ethiopian Jews and Druze have in common? – Jewish identity.

A Temple Mount Moment

I had the pleasure of guiding a young couple of "Noahides" today. Dr. Wilson was a Christian pastor of a community in the US before he parted ways with them for his new spiritual quest. He asked me to accompany him up to the Temple Mount among some other Jerusalem sites.

I first immersed myself in the mikvah (ritual bath) and made sure to meet halachic (religious) requirements before entering the holy Mount.

We proceeded to the long line waiting at the entrance. There was a large group of yeshiva students who were, not surprisingly, being made to wait for hours as the tourists flitted past them to the Mount. The "selection" sends religious Jews to one side for close inspection before being permitted to proceed. They must assure the police that they will not do anything of a "Jewish nature" on our holiest site. It may upset the Muslims. I can never get used to this shameful scene.

To escape the Israel police selection and interrogation I made sure to wear a cap and hide my kippah. This hiding of my Jewish identity worked and we were smoothly admitted as tourists.

As we entered the Mount, I saw the usual scene; tourists, 'Wakf" Muslim officials – the ones who keep an eagle eye out for the stray Jew who slipped through the selection.

We looked harmless enough to the many peering eyes. I noticed the large groups of Muslim women whose job is to accost any Jews who are "caught" looking Jewish. It was eerie to be sure but it was not my first time there.

As we proceeded, I heard a din on the far side of the Mount. It was what I suspected. Arabs were trailing a group of Jews who dared identify as such and were harassing them. The police tagged along to make sure that the Jews didn't pray or do anything similarly provocative and really cause trouble.

I felt a need to connect with these proud Jews. I approached them and offered a "shalom aleichem" greeting. It was surreal. It felt like meeting a fellow human being on a deserted island.

We connected as the Arabs increased their yells and the police nervously ordered us to "keep moving."

We parted and as we went our own way, word apparently spread that there were some Jews who slipped through the selection and needed attention. It did not take long and we were tailed by a group of Arab teens who progressively came closer. Some began to brush up against us testing their limits. My guests were petrified. The police were busy making sure that Jews didn't pray so we were on our own. I was about to shove one of the teens away as an older Arab came on the scene and ordered the youth away from us.

The pack left us and we proceeded alone. My guests were in shock and I was shaken too. After walking in silence, I turned to Dr. Wilson and his wife and said, "I am ashamed of myself. I just left a group of Jews who were unafraid to identify as such in this hostile, threatening place. I avoided that by passing as a non-Jew. That was wrong." At that point I removed my cap, exposing my kippah and let my ritual fringes flow outside my pants.

As we continued to walk towards the exit, I received looks of hate from the Arabs that we passed. Dr. Wilson asked that we stop for a moment.

He was tearing and needed to say something. "Shalom, my entire life I thought how I will be certain that I recognize evil as opposed to good. I always wanted to stand for good. Today I stand with you and your people. What prayer is appropriate?"

The three of us said the "Shema" together.

Am I Not Jewish?

As a tour guide, I am always happy to make new work connections. Self-employed guides, especially Shabbat observers, constantly seek new work opportunities and I heard that a particular company was hiring.

The company was one of the largest that operated "Birthright" groups. Ten days and nights with US college students is exhausting, but it is ten days of work.

Beyond the work, Birthright groups are an opportunity to do good for the Jewish people. It is a chance to teach and inspire Jewish students for ten precious days before they return to the Jewish wasteland most come from.

Constantly bombarded by anti-Israel propaganda, being Jewish is just not cool on campus. For the first time in their lives, they are in a place where they are the majority and all of their friends are Jewish. It is an opportunity to really make a difference.

They agreed to interview me in their office outside of Tel Aviv. It was on the day of the "fast of Esther." I was asked to wait for my interviewer and seated comfortably surrounded by busy young people and the familiar buzz of office activity filled the air. In the spirit of Purim, I was offered a "hamantash." I thankfully declined, explaining that I was fasting. She looked puzzled and asked why?

I said, "the fast of Esther."

At this point the general buzz came to a halt. It seemed that the whole room and beyond were staring at me. Here was a strange phenomenon. They had no idea of what I was talking about.

I continued waiting for my interviewer as the office buzz slowly returned. I was called into a room where a nice young lady greeted me and began the interview. They were the kind of questions I expected as a tour guide; experience, strengths etc. Then she stretched her neck a bit and looked at the top of my head.

She hesitated and asked apologetically, "Tell me, would it be a problem for you to lead the group on Friday night to a pub in Jerusalem and have your phone available for possible calls?"

"Yes, it would," I said.

She suggested that this company would not be a good fit for me.

I agreed and stood up to leave. I was disturbed; not because of the long trip from Jerusalem for naught and not for not getting the job. I felt terrible for the poor students.

To finally come to Israel – to Jerusalem, and spend their only Shabbat here in a pub? I walked out with these disturbing thoughts. I just had to return and talk to the boss.

I reentered the building and asked to speak with the general manager. I was graciously seen into a very impressive office and offered a seat.

He asked how could help me.

I said, "It's not me that I would like you to help, but the Jewish students in your care."

I described the exchange I had with his employee.

His demeanor became a bit less friendly as he assured me that his company knows how to ensure Jewish continuity. They have their methods. Not to worry or question.

I said, "Don't you think that they have the same pubs with the same beer and music where they come from? Should they not be exposed to something different on their only Shabbat in Jerusalem? Many wonderful families would love to invite them for a Shabbat meal and a real Jewish experience."

At this point he became annoyed and cut me off. Gone were the smooth corporate manners. He leaned forward, his facial color deepening and voice rising. He asked me if I did not think that he was Jewish?

I said, "If your mother is Jewish, then according to Jewish law, you are too."

At this he fairly exploded. "What! Is it only my DNA?"

I responded, "What else?"

He rose and yelled, "I speak Hebrew. I serve in the army!"

I observed, "Don't the Druze soldiers do as well?"

Now he pointed an accusing finger at me and said, "You are

Neturei Karta!" (Jews in Hasidic dress who openly support Israel's worst enemies.)

I have been called many things, but that was a first. If the whole thing weren't so sad, it would be hilarious. I returned to Jerusalem with a sad heart.

Pity the ignorant in the hands of the arrogant.

Berlin!?

Almost one hundred years ago, a great man prophesied. Rabbi Avraham Yitzchok Hakohen Kook often found himself at the center of continuing controversy as chief rabbi of Eretz Yisrael. He was an original thinker and revolutionary in his synthesis of the values of the land of Israel, the people of Israel and the Torah. In his time, the Jewish world was divided into distinct camps.

Some identified with the Torah and a lifestyle that enshrined isolated community life in the Diaspora. Life outside the local community was not contemplated. The Jewish people as a Nation with a land was at best a faded memory.

Ensuring their unchanged lifestyle wherever they happened to live at the time, protecting their people and local community against the threats of a menacing world was their sacred task.

With the modern era and the "emancipation" in the late eighteenth century, there arose an awareness amongst some, of the idea that a Jewish Nation and Jewish Land are part of being Jewish.

Some Jews embarked on "Reforming" the faith with their Christian neighbors as their model. Some Jews dedicated themselves to Socialism and Communism. Others clung to a grudging acceptance in their countries and became zealous patriots. Some developed a Jewish identity that stressed secular / Socialist culture, preserving the Yiddish language and literature. Some stressed the cosmopolitan or humanitarian mission of Judaism. Still, others sought the most direct way out of it all – through the church.

With all the twists and turns in this modern era, Jewish history found itself in an identity storm and at a crossroads. Two dominant movements emerged from the turmoil and vied for leadership of the next phase of Jewish history.

The Agudah movement and allies in the "old world" fiercely defended the status quo. What was, must be.

A sovereign Jewish Nation, Land, or people were ideas that

were seen as a threat to an existence so jealously protected for so long.

Then there were the Zionists who rebelled against what was, and sought a "new Jew", sovereign and proud in his own country, working and defending the Land and speaking his own language.

In rejecting the status quo of the degrading Diaspora, they also cut their ties to the thing that assured Jewish existence during the long exile. A Jewish Nation and Land, but without Torah!

No longer will the Jewish people be a nation that dwells alone but a "normal" one, accepted by the family of peoples. This was their proclamation, and they were confident that the Jewish future was theirs.

The two camps glared at each other from distant corners.

Unlike most of the rabbinic world, Rabbi Kook had a great appreciation for the young idealistic pioneers and dreamers. He shared a part of that dream and worked with them while trying to teach them why the Torah needed to be a part of their vision.

Rabbi Kook drew criticism from the rabbinic establishment. How could a rabbi associate with sinners and scoffers?

Rabbi Kook responded to them in a famous letter in which he asked them, "Who will teach them if not me?" He then turned to his pioneer friends and made a dire prediction.

He warned them that if they continue to be divorced from the Torah, their children will reject the very Land of Israel for which they sacrifice.

This prophetic warning came to mind when I listened to a radio talk show this morning. The host is a well-known Leftist. The caller was from Berlin, who left Israel because she objected to the "politics, racism, culture, and corruption in Israel."

"There needs to be a civil war in Israel to defeat the forces of darkness!"

Her grandchildren are native German speakers and she enjoys the culture of Germany.

The proud caller from Berlin is a "Sabra", native born Israeli. Her father was a pioneer and fighter for the land and her family is the Israeli equivalent of the "Daughters of the Revolution."

The host was appalled that she abandoned Israel – and for Germany!

He asked her if it does not bother her that her grandchildren are raised in the language used to order our people into the gas chambers?

"What happened to you," he yelled at her!

"You and I agree on most political issues in Israel, but not this! How can you?"

He added, "I am jealous of the 'National Religious' youth (the students of Rabbi Kook's legacy). I do not agree with their politics or religious beliefs, but you will not find them in Berlin."

If you and many like you would remain in Israel, we, the Left, could run the country once again. Instead, you take the easy way out and flippantly abandon a dream.

He could not have described Rabbi Kook's warning any better.

Why Did You Leave Us?

As I scoured the seating possibilities in the waiting area of the US consulate, waiting to process my passport, I sought out what might be the most interesting place to sit.

I chose to sit next to a colorfully robed gentleman with a big gold cross hanging from his neck. I asked him which denomination he belonged to: "Syrian-Catholic," he answered.

I haven't met many of them, to be sure.

He lives in Bethlehem and in the US. He is from Iraq originally, from where his ancient community was born.

There are definitely things to learn from this man, I thought.

I said, "I understand that Christians are fleeing the Middle East?"

He: "Yes they are, unfortunately."

Me: "Bethlehem was once an all Christian city and is now mostly Muslim right?"

He: "It is about half now, but yes, many Christians are selling their homes cheap and leaving."

Me: "You mean the Palestinian Authority has not been welcoming to your community?"

He was not sure how to handle this one. Would he be quoted? Who is this guy speaking with him?

He: "Well, you know the situation... We just want to live in peace with everyone... We were loyal citizens of Iraq and Syria... but now it is all coming apart, unfortunately. Sadly, Christians have no place left in the Middle East."

Me: "Except Israel."

He: "Yes, except Israel."

(I don't know how tolerant *his* church has been to Jews, historically.)

After a moment of silence, he leaned into me and said in a hushed voice, "Why did you leave Bethlehem? It was so good when you were in charge." Everyone got along. Business was very good. There were lots of tourists..."

I answered, "For peace!"

How shall I describe the look he gave me? He did not know if I was being facetious, totally naive, or just plain stupid.

As I let him try to figure it out, I mentioned that it says in the Bible that Ishmael is a "wild person" and shall always be in conflict with everyone.

He understood that I was, in fact, not totally stupid and could be trusted. He opened up a little more and asked, "Why do you think God created Ishmael in the first place?"

This was going to be an interesting discussion.

We did not have an opportunity for a reasoned theological/philosophical discussion, as my number was called, and we parted.

Should I wonder how he sounds when talking to Christians or Moslems about Jews...?

I thought how grateful I was that he was the one living out of a suitcase and speaking in whispers, and not me and my people any longer.

Try The Truth

A group of five far-left activists from the "If Not Now" Jewish organization infiltrated a Birthright group currently in Israel and offered a private tour of Hebron to students in their group.

"Breaking the Silence" did the guiding in Hebron. This group is dedicated to portraying Israel's soldiers in the worst possible light and then taking legal action against them.

"If Not Now" seeks to "end American Jewish support for the occupation." They launched a new campaign this week called "Not Just A Free Trip." It uses "a diversity of methods" to teach Birthright participants about "the daily nightmare of Occupation."

They infiltrate Birthright groups and influence the other participants by offering them tours and other activities without Birthright's permission.

The above story appeared today. It seems that Birthright free trips to Israel are being used as a Trojan horse by self-hating Jews to poison the minds of the students on Birthright.

Birthright is funded by well-meaning Jews whose aim is to preserve Jewish identity and pride amongst Jewish students constantly fed anti-Israel propaganda. Birthright is basically a Liberal organization, careful about not being perceived as too "partisan" or even too "Jewish." I know because I guided these groups on a number of occasions. I am no longer asked to do so, since I am blacklisted. I broke those rules some years ago.

I recall clearly the morning that I was scratched from the Birthright list. It was just after "Oslo" when one morning the general manager showed up to see for himself the guide who dared to question the wisdom and legitimacy of the accords made with arch terrorist Arafat and his gunmen.

It was Mr. Brug himself, the brother of the then prime minister Ehud Barak (who offered Arafat 97% of Judea, Samaria, and the Golan to Syria) who came to observe and question me. (I wonder how he got that plum job.) In answer to his questions, I did not veer from the truth and so paid the price.

The political commissar was outraged. From that morning, Shalom Pollack has never worked for Birthright.

I recall this today as I read about the spoiled brats who used Birthright as a vehicle for bashing Israel. I thought to myself, how ironic, they compromise on the truth and now they must invent the tools to fight lies.

I would suggest to Birthright, just try the truth.

Let's make our young people proud and give them the tools to tell it like it is. The facts are on our side. Use them.

I guarantee great results.

Blinders Off

Two weeks ago, I was asked to guide a group of US international law students from Valparaiso University. They were on a study tour to learn about the "conflict" in classrooms and on the ground.

I assumed, correctly, that their staff, both their hosts and their accompanying teachers, were pretty much what one finds on Liberal campuses these days.

They probably did not know what they were getting into when I was asked to provide some balance to their very politically correct experience in Israel.

I was allotted one and a half hours of their ten-day program to present the "Jewish nationalist side."

They were studying the controversial "Shimon Hatzadik" neighborhood, or as most of the world calls it, "Sheik Jarrah" neighborhood. It had been one of those robust Jewish neighborhoods for generations before the Jordanian army chased the residents from their homes in the Arab assault on Jerusalem of 1948.

This famous Jewish area (home to the 2,300-year-old tomb of the great Shimon Hatzadik) was one of four contiguous neighborhoods that were turned "Judenrein" by the Arab onslaught in the Independence war of 1948.

This particular neighborhood has recently grabbed headlines because Jews are slowly returning to their confiscated properties into which Arabs have been squatting.

There have been a number of well publicized demonstrations launched by Arabs and Israeli Leftists, protesting the "Jewish settler take over" of "Palestinian areas." It was this "classic Israeli injustice" to the "Palestinians" that these students were told about.

Similar to all such cases, the Arab Left presented their claims to the courts. After years of adjudicating, all the courts found that the trespassers had to leave the properties.

When I met my group, it was this background information

that I presented. I am used to guiding groups that are not always fully informed and though these were international law students, I expected that their teachers did not offer the background I provided in understanding the struggle between the "religious settlers" and the "Palestinians." I also suspected that though they had to provide some balance to their ten-day program, they were not going to be thrilled to have their students exposed to this new material.

Indeed, as I spoke, I could see surprise and curiosity on the part of the students and the uncomfortable body language of their teachers.

When I finished my introductory remarks, there was silence. It was broken by one student who asked quite incredulously, "If these 'settlers' move to the 'Palestinian' areas, then how can there be a two-state solution?"

I answered, "They do not accept that 'solution.'"

When she absorbed this iconoclastic idea, she asked me, "Then what is the solution? What is your solution?"

I said, "I actually do believe in a two-state solution." She and the rest were confused.

"Yes," I said. "One Jewish state here, and one ('Palestinian' if you will) across the river in Jordan, which has a 75% 'Palestinian' population where they share the same language, religion, culture and blood relations. The king's family are foreigners, brought to the throne from Arabia by the British after the first world war. It is an artificial kingdom hated by most of its subjects who are 'Palestinian.'"

The new info produced a buzz among the students and squirming in their seats by their staff.

The same student did not relent. She asked, "Why do Jews want to live in this Palestinian area?"

I answered, "Why not?"

I explained that Jews live anywhere they choose all over the world. Why should they be restricted in Jerusalem? Arabs live in Jewish areas all over Israel and no one challenges their right to do so. I added that legally, the issue is one of real estate law and trespassers are evicted. There was no question about the law in this case.

When one student suggested that there might indeed be a legal question, a teacher had no choice but to acknowledge that the courts were fair.

The issue, I explained, is at its core, a national/religious one that goes beyond the letter of the legal/real estate issue.

Either you accept the idea of Jews living in a Jewish state of their own and entrenching their presence or you do not. If you are a Jewish nationalist, you believe that is exactly why we returned to our land. If you are an Arab or identify with the Arab narrative, then you probably reject that idea. There are few neutral views on the subject.

I was satisfied that I was able to bring some important facts and understanding about the Jewish side that gets so little attention. I knew that by not being politically correct, but insisting on teaching the facts, I might pay a price.

And so it was. The Israeli company that brought the students over and hired me for the short tour wants to please their paying clients and hopes for repeat business. The staff was not enamored by me. I dared to rip off the blinders that they laboriously placed on the eyes of their students. And so I was told not to expect another call from them. It wasn't the first time and probably will not be the last.

Despite the price I have paid for the truth over the years, I have not missed even one meal, thank God.

Do Not Fear Them

Tzipi Hotovely, Israel's deputy foreign minister, drew criticism for an observation of hers that she shared with the public. Stating that Israel is an embattled people that lives with the constant threat of annihilation and with daily terror, she suggested that the American Jewish experience is the opposite.

"Most American Jews do not opt for a military career today and do not know the danger of being killed by an armed enemy (as a soldier or as a civilian) and so it is hard for them to place themselves in Israeli boots." Many were unhappy with this statement. In fact, growing up in America, I never met a Jewish soldier.

As the "great generation" of American-Jewish WW2 veterans and Holocaust survivors leave us, appreciation for what it means to literally defend oneself is dissipating.

It is a new world in which love of one's country and traditions face relentless assault. This is the rule on campus where Jewish students stand helpless in the face of anti-Semitic professors and timid, apologetic Jewish "leaders" who would rather invite an Arab terrorist to speak than a strong and outspoken leader such as Ms. Hotovely.

Her Jewish critics in the US and Israel share much in common.

- They are still loyal to the mantra, "land for peace" after it has proven to be a disaster.
- They share a dislike for the "settlers" who are seen as the main impediment to political realism and "peace" with our "well-intentioned" neighbors.
- They are wary of "too much" Bible or Judaism taught in our schools, exposure to Jewish prayer and holy sites.

One former extreme Left minister of education, Shulamit Aloni, tried to ban the book of Joshua in Israeli schools because she said it was about "conquest," which is "not one of our values."

They are not concerned that thousands of Jewish girls marry Arabs (and convert to Islam). It's a private issue.

Multiculturalism and integration are good. "Tribalism" is bad. As Yitzchak Rabin's wife, Leah, said, "I would rather my grandchild marry an Arab than a settler." They fight for the tens of thousands of Muslim/African illegals to remain in Israel, even as they terrorize Jews in poor neighborhoods like south Tel Aviv who desperately demand their removal. They support the tens of thousands of "Palestinian" women moving to Israel to marry Israeli Arabs under "family reunification" consideration. (Funny how love only enters Israel and never leaves it.)

In the US, Jewish leadership presides over a flock that is predominantly Jewishly illiterate. Their "Jewish" values and position on Israel come from the New York Times, rather than Jewish sources, with which they are not familiar. Sadly, American (non-Orthodox) Jewry is disappearing with over seventy percent intermarriage and rising.

Hotovely was correct when she observed that the Western Wall prayer controversy is, in fact, a political one that the Reform movement is waging against time-honored Jewish tradition and law. The media covers the monthly demonstration of the women wearing tallit and tefillin at the Wall. Do these same women visit the holy place when the cameras are gone? I wonder if they wear tallit and tefillin at home?

Jewish leadership in the US today is made of the same stuff as the court Jews surrounding FDR who sold out Europe's Jews during the Holocaust. They would not rock their comfortable boat by protesting and thus making it a "Jewish war." These same "leaders" were willing to make lots of noise and be arrested for "civil rights" a decade later. That was a cause worth rocking the boat for!

The same leadership ignored the plight of imprisoned Soviet Jewry until a "radical" orthodox rabbi put it on the front pages and it could no longer be shoved under the rug. How the "Jewish leadership" hated him for that! He exposed and embarrassed them into addressing the issue.

The same leadership turned their backs on Jonathan Pollard, victim of extreme legal abuse and anti-Semitism. They were happy to let him rot in jail forever as they condemned him in their pathetic attempts to prove that they were "good Americans."

Ms. Hotovely, do not fear them! They don't count.

A Jew's Passion

Ateret Cohanim members filed eviction lawsuits against dozens of families in Al-Hawa ("Yemenite village") on the pretext that 100 years ago the land belonged to a Jewish charity that cared for the Yemenite poor of Jerusalem. Their purpose is clear: to take over the charity and demand in its name the evacuation of families who have lived in the compound for decades without question.

Allow me to clarify the above press release from Peace Now. Ateret Kohanim is an organization whose mandate is to return Jews to properties in Jerusalem that were once Jewish but illegally occupied by Arabs (due to intimidation, pogroms and war). Peace Now is an organization whose mandate is to prevent Jews from returning to these properties in Jerusalem or in any other part of Eretz Yisrael. They are mirror images of each other.

Biblical Ishmael and Yitzchok were mirror images of each other as were Eisav and Yakov. They were actually less so than Ateret Kohanim and Peace Now. Those who opposed our forefathers had redeeming qualities as pointed out by our sages.

Eisav and Ishmael were also not Jews. They had their own interests and futures to build. They had no reason to champion their adversarial brothers who were in competition for their father's attention and for the family name.

Peace Now, however, is "Jewish," yet their passion is how to minimize the Jewish presence in our land and aid those who dream to dispossess us. This is done with very generous funding from our European "friends." The poisonous coalition of European anti-Semites, Arab enemies and self-loathing Jews are the spokes in the wheels that turn Peace Now.

When Jonathan Pollard, a proud Jewish patriot who has sacrificed thirty years of his life for the security of his people, comes home, God willing, there will be Ateret Kohanim types there to warmly greet him. There will be no Peace Now supporters waiting to greet him.

When Jews are killed by Arabs, Ateret Kohanim types feel the pain of each victim.

Peace Now has other priorities and concerns. They have more important "victims" to worry about.

Their compassion and pain are reserved for our enemies.

How do Jews fall so low?

5 / 2018

Kaddish

Arab students at Jerusalem's Bezalel Academy of Arts and Design hang black signs commemorating the sixty-one Hamas dead at Monday's bloody Gaza border protest.

The above is an item in today's news. On the same day in Tel Aviv, a group of Jews wearing black inscribed the names of these Hamas terrorists and lit candles for them.

And still on the same day, Jews in London gathered to recite kaddish for the souls of the Hamas terrorists who assaulted Israel.

I am not disappointed in Arab university students who bite the hand that educates and feeds them. We encourage it. As far as they are concerned, the Jews who coddle them are fools. Why not take advantage and express the hate you feel?

And the sensitive kaddish reciters in London? I don't recall such a gathering of London Jews for Jewish victims of Arab murder. Apparently they have only limited room in their hearts for mourning.

Israeli public opinion is very far from the type of Jews at our universities who coddle our enemies.

And the pious kaddish sayers in London? Their own kaddish is clearly written on the wall. Their kind never lasted long in Jewish history.

Welcome Welcome Home!

Thank the Lord that we have been privileged to see this day. We have been waiting thirty-five long years for the wonderful news that Jonathan (Yonatan) Pollard has come home! He landed in Israel today with his wife, Esther. They are home at last!

Most of us are familiar with the saga of Jonathan; how he provided Israel with information vital to its security.

We are aware of the unjust, brutal, dehumanizing and anti-Semitic treatment he has endured all these long years. We know how the US justice system was weaponized against the rights, body and soul of one Jew who helped Israel when the US committed to supply Israel with the same vital information. They reneged (Casper Weinberger, Secretary of Defense, son of *meshumadim* (left Judaism), was anti-Israel) and Jonathan could not just stand by. He had to act for his people.

We are aware how Israel turned its back on him and broke its promise to protect him. They dutifully turned him over to the vengeful US authorities when he sought the promised sanctuary in the Israel embassy. The betrayal continued for long decades.

Shockingly, an Israeli agent came to his cell and suggested that he commit suicide for everyone's sake. His former handler who encouraged him, Rafi Eitan, told his wife Esther that he was sorry that he did not shoot Jonathan and thus avoid the ensuing imbroglio.

The American Jewish community (except for a handful like "Young Israel") disavowed and condemned him, fearing accusations of dual loyalty.

Jonathan endured terrible physical and mental anguish, yet did not lose his sanity or his faith. In fact, he began to observe Torah commandments while in prison, and paid a steep price for his loyalty to kosher and Shabbat laws. His health was always very poor and he never received proper treatment, yet he never surrendered.

Israel's former chief rabbi, Rabbi Mordechai Eliyahu, visited him frequently. The rabbi was not in good health, yet made the arduous trips to see him. Yonatan pleaded with him to not come due to the rabbi's health. Rabbi Eliyahu said that he never met a man with stronger faith than Yonatan, and "adopted" him as his son. He said that he shares his soul with Joseph, who was also thrown into a pit and betrayed.

Scanning the Jewish scene, it was apparent that the Jews who stood up for Yonatan came almost exclusively from within the "national religious" community, especially its youth. They were the ones who demonstrated, hung up posters and prayed for our brother Yonatan.

As a participant in the movement to free Yonatan, I often met Jews who felt he deserved what he got or just were not interested. I was amazed and saddened by this. I just could not understand; so much darkness and callousness.

Synagogues that I have attended refused even a public prayer for our suffering brother. They felt it was a "right wing" issue – too political. Haredim felt that it was not their issue. He worked for the Zionists and it wasn't their business. Secular Israel was not interested.

For years I wore a T-shirt with the face of Yonatan demanding his freedom. (I kept the shirt for my grandchildren.) Many thought I was silly or weird. Others appreciated it, but would not dare follow my example. I worked to put up signs and placards. I attended demonstrations and meetings. We were a small group.

God bless the enthusiastic young people who never tire. These are the same beautiful youths who stood up for Gush Katif, Amona and protested terror killings. Belittled and demonized by the respectable "mainstream," it's the same elite, time and again, who don't forget what it means to be a committed Jew, as is Jonathan.

Welcome home, Jonathan. We need you here!

My Heroes

Before I discuss the historic changes in Israeli politics taking place today, I would like to tell you about a special visit I made with a group that I guided. Yesterday, we visited a place called "Maoz Esther" (Esther's Fortress).

Esther Gallia, mother of seven, was murdered in a drive by shooting by "Palestinian" Arabs in 2006 near her home in Samaria. Maoz Esther, near the site of the murder, was subsequently established in her memory. The residents of Maoz Esther did not seek permission from the authorities to build it.

Since the 1993 Oslo calamity, no such permission has been granted to Jews. At the same time, thousands of Arab homes and infrastructure are built contrary to all official government zoning laws, with almost no official response. Jews are aware of their embedded disadvantage vis-a-vis Arabs when it comes to enforcing the law in the "territories."

Maoz Esther is a few shacks, including a synagogue (which is waiting for a roof). In one shack lives eight teenage girls. In another one just a few hundred meters away live some teen-age boys. Some call these young people "hilltop youth."

The boys herd sheep and receive classes from educators. Their daily presence in wide-ranging areas creates a visual Jewish presence beyond their community, thus securing maximum land for the Jewish people. If they were not there, the Arabs would quickly move in and yet another parcel of the Land of Israel would be lost. Their aim is to prevent this. The boys keep a sharp eye out for local Bedouin intruders as they guard their own and the girl's shacks.

The girls, up at the crack of dawn, divide their time between farming, working in neighboring communities, housekeeping and study.

I saw a large pile of debris lying next to the path up to their shack. They explained that every few months, after the police demolish their shack (and brutally drag them out of their beds in the middle of the night), the girls pile the ruins in one spot. To me it looked like some sort of monument. Then they rebuild. I thought, one day that pile will be a monument to Israel's great folly: Instead of persecuting these idealistic youth they should be given every assistance and a medal.

Alas.

Ahuvia Sandak lived in the boys' shack and fulfilled his dream, following his father and grandfather in settling the land of Israel. They faced their challenges and now it was his turn to do so.

A few months ago, Ahuvia was killed when a chasing police car rammed the one he was in. The car flipped and Ahuvia was killed. He was suspected of throwing stones at Arabs. The police and the media are now covering up the incident and preventing an investigation.

During decades of daily Arab stone throwing at Jewish vehicles causing numerous casualties, there has never been a case of hot pursuit and ramming. This determination is reserved only for enemy number one, the "hilltop youth." I met them. They are the best we have.

Now for current Israel politics. In contrast to my visit at Maoz Esther, the Israeli political establishment and media eagerly await the words of Mansour Abbas of the Ra'am party (Muslim Brotherhood). Since half of the Jewish politicians will not sit with the other half to form a government due to reasons of personality and ambition, it falls to the Muslim Brotherhood to choose which government will rule the Jewish state. This is a first in Israeli politics.

The media and political establishment are preparing public opinion to accept this as not just an unexpected result of a democratic election, but welcome progress. For the first time, vying for the agreement of Hamas's supporters is heralded as a positive development.

The youngsters holding onto the land of Israel represent the opposite. Their values have not changed from their fathers. With determination and unchanged innocent faith in our people and country, they are saying "the king has no clothes" no matter how many insist otherwise. That is why they are my heroes.

3 / 2021

Ahuvia

Ahuvia Sandak, 16, lived in Bat Ayin, a village in Judea. He was born in Gush Katif and left in his mother's arms when his family was expelled from their home by Israeli forces. Their home was given to Hamas – for "peace and security" we were assured.

Ahuvia was killed in a car he was riding in with friends. His car was rammed from behind by an unmarked police vehicle. The police were in hot pursuit of alleged Jewish stone throwers at Arabs.

Arab stone throwing at Jews is a round the clock phenomenon. The media, politicians and security people treat it simply as bad weather. However, the police and secret service lie in wait for a Jew to dare to throw a stone at an Arab. That would certainly cause the Arabs to be angry and lead to "instability." That threat must be prevented at all costs!

An entire section of the secret service (The "Jewish section") devotes huge resources to get their hands on one of those illusive public enemies.

No one was allowed at the scene of Ahuvia's death; not journalists and not members of Knesset (Smotrich). What were the police hiding? His family and friends demanded that the police officers involved be seriously questioned. The peaceful demonstrators were brutalized by the same police that wanted the whole thing put to rest.

"Honenu" lawyers are on the job. Yet another whitewash was feared, with the full cooperation of the media. There is little hope for transparency and justice when it comes to "settlers."

Youths who look like Ahuvia are in the crosshairs of Israel's secret service and police. He was young, he lived in the "territories," had flowing side locks and wore a big kippah. He had that look that invited constant harassment and worse.

Stones have killed many Jews. That isn't news, that's life in the "territories." Left wing politicians, academia and journalists tirelessly point out that the "settlers" should be aware of the dangers of living in "illegally occupied territories."

The half million Jews there don't expect preferential treatment. They don't expect applause for living on the Israeli frontier protecting the rest of Israel with their bodies. They would be satisfied if the many Jewish victims of Arab attacks engendered the same police concern as when an Arab is victim to the extremely rare Jewish stone.

They would be happy if the police did not stage situations using "agent provocateurs" and disguised police to entrap Jews and arrest them.

They would be happy to be treated like the Arabs.

Duma

A young man with a wife and baby faces life in prison. Serious doubts have been raised in regard to his conviction.

Here are the facts: In July 2015, in the Arab village of Duma in Samaria, a home was firebombed resulting in the death of three. Graffiti in Hebrew was scrawled on the walls of the house.

The special "Jewish section" of the Secret Service swooped down on a number of "hilltop youths." The usual suspects are continually harassed and provoked by the "Jewish section" who are under great pressure to prove that the huge investment in them shows results. They were going to "get their man" no matter what.

The accused has not been identified by a witness on the scene. His wife testifies that he was with her that entire night. The handwriting on the wall is not his.

The authorities arrested and tortured him. The courts permitted torture on the basis of the Secret Service's claim that he was a "ticking bomb" and information was needed immediately in order to prevent an imminent crime.

This was clearly untrue; a ruse to gain the court's permission to isolate him from legal representation and torture the young man undisturbed. This they did for days and nights demanding a confession. He and a number of young people including minors who live in proximity to Duma were rounded up, intimidated, interrogated, and tortured. One of the minors could not bear it anymore and agreed to identify Mr. Ben Uliel as the culprit.

Suffering severe beatings and the threat of continuing torture, Uliel agreed to admit to the crime. He was ordered to "reenact" the crime and was taken to the scene by the same man that personally tormented him for days and nights. The law forbids the interrogator to be present at the reenactment of the crime. It was ignored.

Knowing that he must satisfy the expectations of his tormentor, he played along.

They brought him to the burnt-out house and he agreed that he threw the fire bomb into the house after opening up the window, exactly as his torturers insisted had happened.

Consider the following: The targeted house is in the middle of the Arab village. Why would an arsonist want to target a house in the middle of the village and thus endanger himself and the operation by making his way through the entire village before and after the attack? Wouldn't it be safer to target an exterior house?

In that same village, prior to this attack, there were multiple incidents of firebombing. These were internal clan conflicts that were initially blamed on Jews but were proven false.

Is it not possible that this was another one of internecine violence and mutual firebombing?

The surviving family member, five years old at the time of the incident, told his grandfather recently (who told a news outlet) that he remembers not one but three men outside the house who doused his parents with gasoline and then lit them. This is a totally different version from what the authorities claim.

To date, a young man is languishing in a high security jail as his wife and daughter endure their hell. Other than his confession under torture, there is no evidence, yet the court sent him to suffer in jail under severe conditions.

Everyone is happy. They finally got their "hilltop youth" and aren't letting go.

Is this really happening or will we wake up very soon as the Psalmist writes: "As if we were dreaming?"

For Shalom

As I stood for the two-minute Holocaust memorial siren, my mind flooded. As the wail winded down, I slowly left dark thoughts as I reminded myself where I am; that I have children and grandchildren in our Jewish country.

This time of year, in Israel, is a time of peaks, dips and hairpin turns of the soul. Remembering the Six Million, Memorial Day for the fallen of our finest young people, and finally Independence Day. We are living miracles.

Tragically, it was on this Holocaust memorial eve when, again, an Arab used his car with Israeli license plates to kill Jews in Jerusalem; two special young people who were planning to raise a beautiful Jewish family.

Shalom Sherki, son of a popular rabbi/teacher, was a model person. Too many words of praise are heard for too many murdered sweet Jews. His fiancé, who he protected with his body, is fighting for her life.

There is an increasing number of concrete barriers at bus and train stops in Jerusalem, as Arabs use their Israel licenses as a weapon with which to kill Jews.

Similarly, the extensive building of bomb shelters near Gaza and the "security fence" along Israel's "border" with the Palestinian Authority have created the "fortress Israel" we now live in.

Who dreamed we would be cringing behind concrete at bus stops in our beloved capital? Is this the best we can do? Are we doomed to look with fear upon every vehicle, wondering if the driver is friend or foe?

Sadly, this new reality has been accepted as part of life, much as daily stone throwing. We get used to things that healthy people never should have to tolerate.

Shimon Peres called it "the price of peace." It wasn't always thus. We stand for moments of silence, with thoughts of "never again" and, "may their blood be avenged."

And what of the blood yet to be spilled? More concrete?

More moments of silence? Who will say, "Enough!" Who will put a stop to the madness – to the desecration of God's people, of His name!

These thoughts filled my mind as I sat on the bus today. Alongside the seats that face each other are signs forbidding from resting of one's feet on the opposite seat. (I often wonder why this instruction is necessary.) When I see a young person put his dirty shoes on the opposite upholstery, I direct his attention to the sign. Sometimes they comply and sometimes I get the Israeli shrug.

Today I saw a young man rubbing his shoes into the opposite seat. I nodded to him, hinting that he should find a more appropriate place for his shoes. He made a disparaging, loud gesture. Probably because he was an Arab, people did not want to "get involved" as they dug their noses deeper into their phones or rose to change their seats.

Today Jews fear Arabs. It wasn't always this way.

The Arab continued to scoff, "Is this your bus? Why do you care?" He continued to dig his shoes into the upholstery and our Jewish faces into the dirt. He was enjoying his victory over the Jews.

"It is my country and so I care!" is what I thought, but I knew that if I made an issue, I would anger lots of Jews on the bus who just wanted to get home safely. I feared they would yell at me and thus cause a real desecration of God's name and national shame. So, I unhappily relented, and the Arab kept his dirty shoes on the seat, and in our face. This, just twenty-four hours after our holy, sweet Shalom was murdered by another Arab in Jerusalem.

We hide in our phones and behind barriers. It wasn't always this way.

When will we "tear down that wall" and press "restart?" I pray that we remember why He brought us to this place with miracles; for the day when we stand tall again and hallow His name. I pray for the many Shaloms, who deserve better.

Letter To Yad Vashem

D ear Ms. Uria,
My name is Shalom Pollack, a veteran, licensed tour guide. Needless to say, I have guided visitors in Yad Vashem on hundreds of occasions.

One of the lesser-known aspects of the Holocaust by the public is the part played by the Grand Mufti of Jerusalem, Haj Amin el Husseini. His role was revealed to the public in a clear way in the former museum, as you are surely aware.

The floor to ceiling photo of the mutually admiring Hitler and Husseini did not need many words of explanation. I have always found that visitors appreciated being exposed to this revelation that the new Yad Vashem decided to remove.

After writing to Yad Vashem a few years ago about this, the reply was, "in the new museum, we place a greater emphasis on the victims than on the perpetrators."

However, just five paces from the now minuscule, well hidden photo of the Mufti and Himmler (no longer the well-known figure of Hitler) in a dark corner is an entire wall of perpetrators, German, not Arab. German sensibilities are still fair game, but not Arab. So much for not emphasizing the perpetrators.

The new museum is a "post Oslo" design and I heard that PLO leader Faisal Husseini ("Oslo was a Trojan Horse") was outraged that his great uncle was exposed, and thus the change was made by Yad Vashem. Whether this is a true anecdote or not, I protest the state of the current misleading Holocaust narrative.

The cover up robs visitors of an important piece of the Holocaust history and is a humiliating concession to the heirs of an ally of Hitler in the extermination of our people.

Is it not the time to restore truth and national pride? I write this letter not for personal gain or for want of better things to do with my time. I just care very much about our people and about truth, especially in an era of devastating moral relativism and Holocaust denial.

Before I make this letter public – as public as I can, I eagerly wait to hear from you that Yad Vashem is going to fix the irresponsible and damaging current display.

With respect,

Shalom Pollack

Yad Vashem replied to this letter, claiming that they "do indeed tell the story of the role played by the Mufti in detail."

They may do so, but far, far fewer visitors confront the information than before, I suspect, by design. The infamous Hitler (now Himmler) / Husseini photo is one fiftieth its previous size and hides in a dark corner hoping to be undiscovered.

I also know that visitors and even local guides of Yad Vashem are not familiar with the chapter of massive Nazi-Arab collaboration. I asked some of the local guides if they explain this aspect of the Holocaust to visitors.

One told me, "No."

Another said, "It's too political."

Another told me she "was not aware of it."

Yet another said, "We are discouraged to do so."

Despite the expected laconic bureaucratic response of Yad Vashem, it is clear to me that my suspicions are indeed correct. I believe that this must be corrected and the picture restored to its former rightful place. Enough sacrificing truth and self-respect upon the altar of political correctness. I will indeed do all I can to make this happen and invite you to join my efforts on behalf of the memory of the Holocaust, the Jewish people, and Israel.

Two Disturbances

The Rosh Hashana before last, a small group of worshipers gathered at the "Kotel Hakatan" (a portion of the Western Wall tucked inside the Muslim Quarter in the Old City). As the shofar was blown, the Muslim neighbors complained to the police about the noise. The law enforcers immediately swooped down on the worshipers and broke up the service, even dragging some away as they prayed the central *amidah* prayer. Brutalized, the group was dragged off to the police station where they were further humiliated. This kind of treatment of religious and nationalist Jews has been the norm for Israeli law enforcement for quite some time.

Each morning at about 4:30 I am roused from my sleep by blaring loudspeakers coming from the Arab village mosque located about a mile from my house. This booming awakening is not just my private concern. When I call the police each morning, I am told that hundreds had called about this disturbance. They tell me, "It is being taken care of, but it can't be solved in one night."

It's been months of almost daily calling. Each time the same bureaucratic procedure. They want to know my name and where I live; the same details repeated as the morning star begins to rise. I complained that it has "been taken care of" for months. Am I doomed to be awoken each morning at 4:30?

Sometimes I am transferred to someone else with greater authority. One told me, "It's their prayers, what do you want? I should accept their prayers." I am made to feel that I am just unreasonable. Or, "It's a very complicated issue."

When Jews blow a shofar on Rosh Hashanah at the Wall, it isn't complicated in the least. It is very clear. Jewish prayers once a year are less tolerable than Muslim prayer five times a day.

Finally, today I received what is clearly the true answer. The man with the higher rank in the room got on the phone to tell me that, "It is dangerous to enter the Arab areas."

So that's it. It is not dangerous to brutalize Jewish worshipers. Well, this is the shameful situation of Israel today. Are we marching, eyes open towards the abyss?

Didn't the prophet say that there will come a time when right will be called wrong and wrong will be called right? The prophets indeed said it was going to be a very bumpy ride. In the Talmud, scholars discuss whether they would, in fact, want to live in the end times with all its difficulties and challenges.

One cannot make sense of the illogical and self-destructive policies of Israeli governments in this last generation.

Did our rabbis expect something like this? Did the Talmud scholars see it coming long ago?

Hate Crime!

Flash! Yet another hate crime! Arab property was allegedly damaged by Jewish youths. The media is enraged. Hate, hate, hate!

How long will these haters, abetted by racist religious fanatics, blemish our democracy?

In the midst of the anti-hate crusade, I ask myself, "When Arabs attack Jews (about a hundred times more often than the opposite) do the Left-wing anti-hate crusaders raise their righteous voices to 'stop the hate crimes'?"

(Spoiler: No, they do not.)

Just yesterday in the "mixed city" of Lod, Arabs mobbed and beat the community rabbi. They brutally dragged him out of his car and severely pounded him in front of his screaming small children. Will the anti-hate crusaders of the Left exhibit outrage?

So far, no. I won't hold my breath.

But wait – Was the brutal attack on the rabbi really a hate crime? Perhaps it was just an everyday dispute between neighbors? Who said there was an anti-Semitic or hate motive?

The police prefer to describe attacks by Arabs against Jews as just another case of violence and do everything not to label them "nationally inspired hate crime."

By acknowledging the growing problem of Arab attacks on Jews, they cannot sweep it under the carpet. The police and courts know the truth but are not willing to recognize a problem that they don't want to recognize and is too great for them to handle, let alone solve. So it doesn't exist.

However, when a Jewish youth spraypaints an Arab property, the entire establishment fully mobilizes against the unacceptable blemish of hate.

Our rabbis designated a special prayer that we recite three times a day. We beseech God to "bring back our true judges and spare us suffering."

Amen.

3 / 2012
Sechel
(Common Sense)

As I entered the club where I work out, I was greeted by Shalom, a member of the Left-wing kibbutz "Ramat Rachel" that owns and runs the facility.

He asked what the meaning of my T-shirt was. It was a depiction of Jerusalem with a famous biblical quote, "For Jerusalem's sake I will not be silent", in Hebrew and English. He thought it was corny at best, perhaps even provocative. I told him that my Christian tourists love it and really identify with the message.

He smirked and said, they have no "sechel" (common sense).

I said, "You may think they have no sechel, but I can tell you that they have lots of heart." Then I added, "Yes there are Jews with so much sechel that they can even empathize with our enemies who want to destroy us."

Former prime minister and chief of staff Ehud Barak once said if he were a "Palestinian," he would also be a terrorist.

On my way out, he stopped me to have a "serious conversation." He must have given some thought to our brief exchange earlier. He said with some exasperation, "we have to pursue peace, no matter the setbacks. There are other people living in this land and they must be accommodated. We are not always right."

I thought that this tired mantra had been put to bed with the terrible price we paid for the Oslo illusions, but no, I was talking to a broken record. I asked what his solution was to the "problem." He said we have no choice but to continue "pursuing peace." There is no other alternative.

Does this mean more conceding of land to "the other people?"
"Yes."

But that did not work. Does he not agree that whenever we abandon land to "them," it always results in blood and fire?

He agreed.

However, he said, "we have no choice."

"But they want all the land. They said so," I reminded him.

"I know," he said.

He then began to explain that there are "extremists on all sides" and we have to work towards a logical fair middle ... The broken record kept turning.

I related to him an interview that I heard on the radio some years ago. It was with Dr. (full of sechel) Yossi Beilin, who was one of the major architects of the Oslo disaster.

Upon mention of his name, my friend stiffened, showing great respect for a hero of the Left.

I recalled that he was asked, "Now that a few years have passed since Oslo and with it, the great upsurge in Arab violence and hatred, do you think it was perhaps not a success?"

His answer is one I shall never forget because it capsulizes the approach of my friend Shalom and the Left.

After a short pause, Beilin responded, "I simply cannot live in a world bereft of hope. There must be light at the end of the tunnel and I am prepared to continue to pay a price but never abandon hope."

My friend totally agreed with the wise words of the great Dr. Beilin. He pondered them with great admiration.

Now why didn't I think of that? Where is my sechel?

Flowers And Candles

Kneeling on a Paris Street, next to the place where hundreds of people have placed flowers and candles to commemorate the victims of Friday's atrocious terror attacks, a French reporter interviews a little boy, maybe four or five years old.

"Do you understand why these people did what they did," the reporter wants to know.

"Yes, because they're very, very, evil. They're not very nice, these bad guys," the boy replies. "You have to be very careful and you have to switch houses," he adds.

"Don't worry," his dad interrupts, gently stroking the boy's head. "France is our home," he declares, "and we're not going anywhere."

The young boy is not calm. "They have guns and they can shoot at us, because they're very evil."

"True, but we have flowers," the father retorts, pointing at the sea of people showing their respect to the victims. "Look, everybody is putting down flowers. That's to fight the guns."

At first the boy is skeptical – "Flowers don't do anything," he says, but his father reassures him that the flowers, together with the candles, protect us from the evildoers. The boy looks relieved as his father gives a satisfying smile to the reporter.

The above is part of an article I read that fits perfectly with the experience that I had yesterday, as I guided a very pleasant group of pastors from Holland.

The theme of the tour was the topographic / strategic and demographic influences on Jerusalem today and tomorrow.

I was to supply some of the essential facts that are vital in order to discuss political and inter communal issues of the city.

We began on "Ammunition Hill", the main site in the battles for Jerusalem in 1967.

I think that some of my guests were surprised to hear that all the neighborhoods that they saw from the strategic, former Jordanian hill, were Jewish, mostly established after 1967 in what were occupied areas by Jordan since 1948.

I explained that 350,000 Jews of Jerusalem live beyond the "Green Line" in areas that their Dutch ambassador would not visit because it was "occupied territory."

They were riveted as they scanned the panorama. I knew that this did not fit their conception of "occupied East Jerusalem."

The expected questions followed as we began to feel a bit more familiar with each other.

"So," I was asked, "what about the illegal and immoral occupation of other's lands?"

They needed a basic lesson of the Arab-Israel conflict.

I explained how there never was a Palestinian state or even a people, not in this area or in any other; how Jordan was an artificial creation on land that was designated for a Jewish state and how it illegally occupied the "West bank" when it attacked Israel in 1948 and lost it to Israel when Jordan again attacked in 1967.

"Why then," I ask, "are anyone's claims to the 'territories' better than ours?"

There was no response, but one man looked rather uncomfortable. I turned to him, "You seem unhappy."

He agreed that he was not. He said, "Do you think it is correct to occupy people's private lands?"

I explained that every Jewish town and village "beyond the Green Line" (about 500,000 people today) was built on government land; land that was once controlled by the Turks, the British, the Jordanians, never by private people.

I asked again, "Why are our claims inferior to anyone else's?"

Again, he could not answer but something was still bothering him. I asked him what it was?

He blurted, "So what about the Arab rights, what about their state? What is your solution?"

So now we are not talking about rights, but rather a solution to the "Palestinian" problem.

How does one answer a question based on emotion and not on facts or logic?

I knew I was about to shock these liberal, politically correct ladies and gentlemen from Europe.

I told them, "They must go."

They asked me to repeat that, as if they could not believe their ears.

I said, "Yes, they cannot live in peace with us. They indoctrinate their children to hate and kill us, so they must leave us and we will help them. In fact, if the world had an honest concern about solving the 'Palestinian problem' they would contribute land and resources to resettle them and not feed their hate fantasies. It would not be difficult."

A good portion of the "Palestinians" would love to leave if they could. Polls bear this out.

This really angered my Dutch guest. He said, "Why don't the Jews find some place to go, like North Dakota." (I would have preferred southern California.)

I explained to him that if the entire reason for a Jewish state was physical safety, that would be a theoretical solution. However, I informed him that I did not leave the USA because I sought security or creature comforts. I left because this is the only land that God commanded me to live in. As clergy, I thought they should have appreciated that.

They finally met a straight-talking unapologetic Jew. Some were in shock.

On the way back to the bus, I asked one of them for his assessment of the Muslim problem plaguing Europe. He agreed that there was a real problem.

"And how to solve it?" I asked.

He said, "We have to hope that the next generation will be better educated and see there are better ways of living together. We must reach out to them and show them a better way. That is all we can do, that is all."

I thought, and if that does not work. There are always flowers and candles.

Such nice, but naive people. Pity.

Enjoy Your Guests

Another Muslim terror attack in Europe; this time Spain – again. No one expects it to be the last one. Western Europe (Eastern European countries refuse to open their doors to Muslims) just does not know what to do with their guests. There is a certain irony and historic justice in the continuing Muslim attacks upon Europe.

For years, when Israel singularly bore the brunt of Muslim terror attacks, Europe pursued a policy of appeasement of Muslim "rage" towards Israel and symphonized with the "Palestinian" cause. They hoped that this would contain Muslim "rage" to Jews only. To this end, they coddled the PLO and treated Israel as the Cinderella of the world.

Those with common sense and an ability to learn from history knew that Israel was just the beginning of a problem. Appeasement of evil has never worked. It is always tempting to kick the can down the road and hope for the best.

Israel was the canary in the coal mine. Europe turned a deaf ear to the rumble of the approaching avalanche. Meanwhile, as Israel was forced to stand alone in its defense against Islamo – fascism disguised as "Palestinian resistance," it was forced to hone its skills of survival and so Israel is today the world's model and instructor in fighting terror as it spreads. Its society is the most resilient in the face of it.

The lessons that Israel has learned in its isolation will have to be learned by a complacent Europe that lost the will to fight for an identity that they have abandoned. They have shackled themselves from dealing with the threat to their civilization. Still, they pour vast sums into anti-Israel organizations in the hope that the monster will be fed and satisfied. Appeasement is still a powerful elixir and difficult to be weaned from.

Spain was once the most powerful country in the world – when it was the center of world Jewry. However, in 1492 they gave the Jews a choice; convert or leave. Overnight, Spain was emptied of its Jews, led by their illustrious leader Don Isaac Abarbanel.

Don Isaac was a friend and advisor to King Ferdinand. As he led the Jews out of Spain, he left a blistering letter for his erstwhile friend. In short, he predicted the swift demise of Spain now that its most vital population was leaving.

Spain sank quickly.

Europe did not want Jews – despite their disproportionate contribution and bringing prosperity wherever they lived.

Dear Europe, you made your choice. You did not want the Jews, so now enjoy your new guests.

Just A Few Stones

As a tour guide I always search for interesting places. Last year, I was excited to organize a tour to Mount Eival atop of which is the recently discovered and excavated "Joshua's altar." This was one of the most amazing biblical archeological discoveries of all time.

When Joshua led the Israelites across the Jordan River into the heart of the Promised Land, he stopped to offer a thanksgiving sacrifice and reaffirm the people's allegiance to God and His Torah.

Mount Eival is in the heart of Samaria, near Shechem, the Biblical heartland that Israel liberated in the 1967 war. Since the government did not take advantage of the victory to expel the hostile population during the war (as Joshua did almost 3,500 years ago), there is a large Arab population in and around Shechem today.

After coordination with various official bodies, including the military, I organized a sizable group to visit this site of monumental historical and spiritual significance.

The night before the big day, I was informed that the military called it off due to "security concerns." Aside from the many practical difficulties this caused me, I was embarrassed and disappointed in our country.

The Jewish country and military were incapable or unwilling to secure one of the most important sites of the Jewish people and Land?

This morning I heard that Arabs of the "Palestinian Authority" (which Israel created in 1993) destroyed parts of Joshua's tomb. Israeli authorities turn a blind eye to a systematic campaign to erase all Jewish historical traces in our land. The list of vanishing historical sites grows as those who challenge Israel's connection to our land can "check another box."

Later in the morning I heard an interview about the erasure of Jewish history. Major General Gershom Hacohen said that he heard a high ranking PA official state that he supports a two state solution. He explained why. He said that if Israel willingly deprives themselves of the cradle of their biblical sites that are in Judea and Samaria, they will be left with Tel Aviv and Haifa. It is at that point that the Jews will have lost all physical connection to their past and roots, the current sovereign will eventually cease to be Jewish and then disappear.

He is a smart Arab. He sees the big picture and knows where the vital battles are fought.

It reminds me of an incident that occurred in an Israeli prison some years ago. It was Pesach and a hardened terrorist witnessed a perplexing scene. He knew that on this day Jews do not eat bread, yet he saw a jailer doing just that. He asked him to explain. The guard laughed and said he was modern and not beholden to events thousands of years ago.

The terror leader had to think about this. The next morning he assembled his jail mates and announced, "We are going to win!" They stared at him waiting for some original strategic analysis.

He told them of his short conversation with the guard and concluded, "they don't respect their own roots and traditions." We do. We will win.

Those who systematically destroy all evidence of our heritage know what they are doing. The Israeli authorities clearly do not. They can't be bothered and perhaps are happy to be rid of the burden of a Jewish history. It's time to move on. It's called post-Zionism.

For some Israelis, the Jewish past is a burden. Didn't Shimon Peres (architect of the Oslo debacle and author of "The New Middle East") like to lecture Jewish students about how history is not important. "We can be a Singapore of the Middle East! Let go of history!"

I can just see Peres and friends rolling their eyes at all the fuss over a few stones on a mountain.

We have a Singapore to build!

8 / 2015
Guiding The Druze

During my career as a tour guide, I have met all kinds of people. Jews and Christians of every stripe, Muslims, Buddhists, Hindus, and probably lots of others I wasn't aware of – but never Druze.

This week I added Druze to my list. It was an interesting experience. The Druze are a religious minority that live in the mountainous areas of Israel, Lebanon and Syria. Their religion is one that broke away from Islam in the eleventh century. Because of the fatal consequences of heresy, details of their faith have been kept hidden from the Muslims and remain a "secret" until today. Only the initiated, "religious" among them are privy to the knowledge. They have their own attire and facial hair that distinguishes them. The "initiated" women too have their own attire.

One may not convert into this secret faith. A small group, they do not have national aspirations and are happy to serve the country they live in. In Israel, they serve with distinction in the Israeli army as they do in the Syrian and Lebanese army. They are hardy agrarian people who defend their honor and rights.

I received a call from an organization called "Im Eshkachech" (If I forget). Their aim is to bring as many Israelis to Jerusalem in order to strengthen their ties to the capital. This week is the one hundred eleventh anniversary of Theodor Herzl's passing and groups were arriving from all over the country for a ceremony on Mount Herzl.

When I spoke on the phone to the one in charge of my Druze group, he said that they definitely want to include the Har Nof neighborhood in their itinerary. They wanted to see where their fellow villager, policeman Zaidan Saif was killed by Muslim terrorists as he was called to the scene of a terror attack in the "Kehilla Benei Torah" synagogue.

Last November, two Arabs who had worked in the Jewish neighborhood, stormed the shul with hatchets, cleavers and pistols. Four men were butchered as they wore their tefillin and tallitot. The Druze officer was stuck down while he eliminated the terrorists.

When I heard the request from the Druze organizer, I realized there was a personal side to this. My cousin, Aryeh Kupinsky, was one of the four victims.

When I shared this with him, there was silence on the other end of the phone. We both knew that this was not going to be a regular tour of Jerusalem.

As I entered the bus and introduced myself, I realized that the women sat in the back and the men in front. Some were dressed in traditional dress and some in regular attire.

We drove straight away to the shul. I had very little time to organize any kind of reception for them, but I was amazed how successful I was at enlisting a number of people who were there during the attack as medical and emergency teams.

As we drove through the neighborhood, I was asked if "Arabs still dare enter the area after the attack?"

I said, "Yes, they still work in the shul where it happened." He had difficulty understanding this but politely said nothing.

An ambulance dedicated to the four victims and the Druze policeman was brought and displayed for them. A medic who was first on the scene addressed the group in perfect Arabic, as he was a Syrian Jew who came to Israel a few years ago. The physician in whose arms Zaidan died called to share her feelings with them.

One of the Druze elders was surprised that there was no guard at the door after what had happened.

Sensible question.

The Jewish hosts mumbled something about the high cost and impossibility of guarding everything all the time.

Silence.

I broke the silence by observing that there are, after all, no guards in mosques. Why should there be in synagogues? At that, both the Druze and Jews snickered, "Of course not, no one threatens them." Only Jews must be on the alert.

Silence again.

I broke it again by suggesting that Kahane was right and waited for their reaction.

They responded in unison, "Of course Kahane was right!".

Druze farmers and Torah scholars – common sense.

After this moving highlight, we continued with the regularly scheduled program.

I had a chance to get to know the Druze. I spoke to young and old, the "initiated" and the regular folk. They don't like being called Arabs. They do not want to be associated with the national (Muslim) enemy and their Muslim neighbors – their neighbors. They have a long and sour history.

I asked the elder what he thought of Christians and Muslims. He said the Christians are at least gentlemen and educated (though I understand that there is plenty of bad blood between them. In Israel, Christians do not threaten them, unlike in Lebanon.

And Muslims? Never to be trusted; barbarians. "I cannot let my daughter loose among them." They fear them because of history, their greater numbers and their growing assertiveness today.

When Israel was born, the Druze were at the very bottom of Arab society. After Israel won its independence, they chose to ally with Israel. They became the envy of all other Arabs – and the object of their hate.

I asked one of the teens, what are you? "I am a Druze in my blood!" This is a proud bunch.

They do not speak Hebrew very well, especially the girls. The men learn it well enough in the army. The women are aware of their deficiency and are somewhat shy because of it.

One teen was very proud to inform me that he studied in a Jewish school for six years and no one even suspected that he is Druze! He was proud to say that he has many Jewish friends.

I noticed that a good number of the teens were into body building. Some of the girls were wrapped in the clothes of the "religious" and others were heavily made up and wore very fashionable attire. I asked the elder what is the meaning of this dichotomy?

He indeed lamented the weakening of tradition among the youth but said each Druze can choose between a secular or religious path. Apparently, there are high expectations and restrictions for the religious and few for the others. It is never easy to commit.

And do the "non-religious" go to heaven? He said the Druze believe that everyone repents and becomes "religious" before death. Simple and reassuring.

I asked him about communal prayer. They pray twice a week, that is, the religious ones do. Only the initiated enter their house of prayer. Their holy book must only be handwritten and very few are permitted access to it.

I asked why their prophet of choice is Jethro, father-in-law of Moshe? Either he did not know or he would not share the secret. Now I really wanted to know! Are they the original Midianites as I have heard said? Again, I was left wondering. Did he know?

They have total respect for their community, religious elders. Their word is law in the villages.

They showed a great thirst for Jewish history and Torah concepts. I guess it is not part of their school curriculum. (How well versed are Israeli Jewish children in their own history?) The elder thirstily wrote down all I was saying. It seemed that the women in the back of the bus were not expected to be taking part in what was going on. They just chatted.

During a break as we were sitting under a tree, I suddenly heard shouting right behind me. One of the older men was attacking one of the bodybuilder teens. He rushed the youngster as he removed his glasses, prepared for what looked like a fight to the death. The younger one did not back down and took his glasses off as well. Both were yelling, cursing and threatening when some of the elders, including a woman and another bodybuilder, separated them. I am pretty sure that "honor" of some sort is what was at stake; very common in the Middle East.

I understood when the elders pleaded with them not to shame the Druze in front of me. They were concerned about the Druze reputation. I was embarrassed for them. They looked at me sheepishly.

Eventually the woman explained to me that the older person thought that the younger was making light of him and disrespecting him. Boy did that launch him!

Now I understand the Druze mentality. When you are a

minority in the Mid-East, you can't afford to be seen as backing down.

When we came to Mount Herzl and the ceremony, the group leader made it clear to the teens that they represented the Druze and he would tolerate no misbehavior. He did not ask, he yelled, gestured and got blue in the face.

Were they such a tough group or was this normal communication? I think the latter. I see it all the time amongst the Muslims.

Indeed, they were the most disciplined group waiting in line. They hardly spoke in deference to their no-nonsense leader (who is a great guy by the way). They wanted to make a good impression.

It was now my turn to feel embarrassed.

The entrance was not administered in perfect order. Surprise?

Groups passed ours as we waited patiently. I demanded that our group be allowed in and was met by a disinterested response. My Druze counterpart was also determined that we enter, now!

He was right. It was a typical Israeli "balagan" – chaos.

I somehow diffused the powder keg and we entered. Raffa, my colleague, and I fought "shoulder to shoulder" for our rights to enter.

I was embarrassed. Israelis should be a light unto the nations.

When we parted at the end of the day, I was made to feel like one of the tribe and now have a place to stay in the Galilee.

Germans And Arabs

O ne of the things I like most about being a tour guide is the opportunity to meet and learn about different peoples and cultures. I guided a group of Catholic Germans led by their pastor. He was quite nice and helpful especially since German is not my mother tongue. The people were elderly and friendly. There were a few sourpusses. I wondered if it was just the way they are, or if it had to do with the surprise of being guided by an Orthodox Jew. We Jews have a right to be paranoid. I am certain that just about all of them had wartime family secrets that they would rather not share.

I normally do not guide German or even Christian groups. That is because I do not work on Shabbat. It is a serious drawback for agents. If I am called upon, it is always because an emergency arose and a guide is needed very quickly. In this case, as the group was leaving Germany, the guide had to back out. Emergency.

All of a sudden, being a Sabbath observer is an "advantage" for the agents. "We want you specifically because you are religious. You are perfect for this particular group, blah, blah ..."

I am always "so flattered." I demanded work and pay conditions that I could never expect if not for the leverage I had in this emergency. I used it. I did not have to work on Shabbat and was paid the salary I requested. The company is a well-known Arab one from East Jerusalem. So here I was guiding Germans for an Arab company. If they could only see me in Brooklyn!

What I found most interesting about this particular experience was my driver. He was a rookie and asked me to please help him on his first job. I was helpful and covered up for mistakes. He tried hard to please. He was an Arab from East Jerusalem and did not know the Galilee very well, and his Hebrew was poor so my limited Arabic came in handy.

The company provided him with a bus that had seen better days. One of the chairs was broken. It seems that the group complained to the company about the bus. The office called the driver and gave him a tongue lashing. He turned pale. His first job and he was getting it from all sides. He was the scapegoat, the lowest on the ladder. Poor guy.

He was very shaken and pleaded with me to please say a good word about him to the group leader with whom he could not communicate. His company was ready to put all the blame on him and throw him under the bus (no pun intended).

I assured him that in my eyes he was a perfect driver and a good man. I made sure that the group leader shook his hand and said some kind words.

On a break as we sat together in the hotel lobby, I asked him, "why is there so much violence in Arab society?"

He gave me a strange answer: "Arabs just want to eat and have good times."

I wasn't sure that he understood my question in my limited Arabic. He then told me that he was so happy to live in Israel where there is law and order, good economy and excellent medical service. His daughter receives dialysis in a Jerusalem hospital, fully paid for by the state.

He posited that his daughter's problem might be a result of his marrying a cousin. I asked him why he did that. He answered, "It's all in the hands of Allah."

When I told him I would not be working on Friday and Shabbat, he was unhappy. He asked, "Will the replacement guide be an Arab?"

I said, "Yes, you will have an easy time communicating." He was now even less happy. In fact, he looked rather distraught.

I asked, "Is that a problem?"

He responded gloomily, "Arabs always make a "balagan" (mess). Unless this was all a big show for my benefit, he really did have reason to be very happy living in a Jewish country and working with a nice Jewish guide rather than an Arab one. I know what he means.

I thought about how life would be in a country where Arabs were the majority. It would be, at best, another failed Arab country. Yes, they are lucky that we are the majority, and he readily admits it. It was an interesting few days.

I Was A Prison Guard

One doesn't always know what duties are expected of a reservist when called up for annual service. I have done a number of things as a reservist but never this: I was to be a prison guard.

There is a huge prison camp next to the Ketziot armor base in the Negev. It holds terrorists where the prisoners live in tents within mini compounds. Guards patrol between the mini camps and watch from guard towers.

There is a kitchen area where the prisoners have their own cooks prepare their favorite foods five times a day. Food was so plentiful that there was bread available for what we called "fax communication." They would write a message and place it in the middle of a ball of dough and then throw it to a neighboring compound. The launch was preceded by a whistle. This sound became part of the ambiance of the camp experience for me. Another staple of the camp atmosphere was the horrible polluting thick black clouds that rose from their heat ovens.

After a long hot ride in an army truck through the desert we finally arrived at Kitziot toward sunset. Just after we were settled in the tents we shared with mates, we were given an informal introduction to our new home for the next three weeks.

All of a sudden it seemed like all hell broke out. The prisoners had coordinated a riot that night, probably to shock and test the fresh reservists. Luckily, the shift before us had not yet left so we did not have to bear the brunt of the action or decide how hard to push back.

They began to burn their mattresses and tents and congregated at the fences, pushing on them menacingly.

The entire camp personnel were called out. We were ordered to follow the lead of others standing opposite the rioters with our weapons at the ready.

I asked myself, "Will I actually pull the trigger on one of the terrorists tonight?" I was armed with rubber bullets and also with live ammunition.

Before things got totally out of hand some of the veterans shot tear gas and rubber bullets into the compounds. The rioters fled, coughing, covering their eyes with wet clothes which seemed pre-prepared.

Just to make sure that they learned some respect for the power of their guards, heavy armored vehicles from the armor camp next door were sent rumbling down the paths between the compounds shaking the ground in their wake.

I understood later that these "riots" were rituals to prove that they were "defiant" of the authorities, and no more.

This was my first night of reserve duty. Was this what to expect for the next three weeks?

It was the first, and last riot that I witnessed. The days and nights passed with the guard duty shifts. A full night's sleep was not part of the deal.

Sometimes I was assigned to foot patrols and other times I was sent up into a tower. Actually, they have no reason to risk their lives in an escape. Conditions were very tolerable.

I was sent up to a guard tower where I was alone for a few hours with my machine gun for company. I always asked myself, "Will there be a situation where I will have to use this weapon?" How would I feel if I actually had to shoot at menacing or fleeing terrorists?

Prisoners were forbidden to touch the fence, though it was never clear to us what the consequence would be for breaking this rule.

We understood that the last thing our commanders want is "action" and so we normally ignored the infraction.

Once on a watchtower, a neighboring tower guard shot his rifle in the air to warn a prisoner away from the fence. He quickly retreated. He dared shoot despite the unofficial policy of looking the other way. We admired him for it.

We were briefed by one of the staff about the people we were guarding. They were terrorists who were arrested while carrying out attacks on Jews or security forces.

They belong to various terror factions and ideologies, from Islamists to Communists. The common denominator was they all wanted to see dead Jews.

They were allowed to choose their tents according to their particular affiliation and ideological indoctrination.

In order to discourage cooperation with the authorities, new inmates will be required to prove their loyalty. They must assault a guard and pay the price that the authorities mete out.

Punishment by the terrorist "committee" is feared much more than that of the IDF. We were shown photos of mutilated prisoners' parts who were suspected of disloyalty. To ensure loyalty and discipline, prisoners are reminded that "we know where your sister lives."

Daily, I watched as lawyers and family members met prisoners at the gate. I suspect that one of the conversations was "How much 'pay for slay' money entered my account this month and how are plans coming along for an abduction of a Jew and a prisoner swap? How many of us will be free in the exchange? Am I on the list?"

The three weeks passed and I was going back to "the world." I have learned how fairly we treat our prisoners under our watch. I shudder to compare how ours are treated by them.

Culture?

O ne can have interesting experiences in post offices where the Israeli cross section meets and waits.

Many Arabs use my neighborhood branch. Today, there were about half Arabs, a quarter, "Olim," recently arrived French Jews whose families originated in North Africa and a smattering of other Jews like me.

The urgency to leave France for Israel is rising Muslim anti-Semitism. I tried to imagine what was going through their minds as they found themselves in the company of many Muslims again. Were they uncomfortable, disappointed, indifferent...?

Now they were in their Jewish country though you would not necessarily know that this morning in the post office.

When some of the Arabs raised their voices and seemed to act as if the Jews were some kind of intrusion, I felt uncomfortable. I was concerned about how our French brothers and sisters might feel. Is this the Jewish country they came to, to escape Muslims?

One middle-aged Israeli sitting in a corner became increasingly agitated as he saw Arabs cutting the line. He grumbled aloud to himself. That was the loudest protest that Jews allowed themselves in the intimidating atmosphere.

One young Arab picked up on this and loudly berated him: "You should have patience; have some 'culture.' We Arabs treat people with respect. We have culture!" The belligerent young man was not challenged.

I felt that this arrogant diatribe, demeaning Jewish culture in our land demanded a response from a Jew. I realised that this wasn't a local incident. It represented far more.

He sat next to me. I turned to him and asked him for all to hear, if the fine Arab culture and respect he is so proud of can be found in Syria, where they slaughter each other? Maybe in Lebanon, Jordan? Iraq, Egypt...?

He, no longer yelling, mumbled, "Those places are different."

Culture?

I asked if he meant then the local "Palestinian" Arab culture of endemic violence and family honor killings?

If looks could kill... But he shut up.

They just hate it when you know the facts and are not afraid to state them.

I hope that our brothers and sisters from France felt better.

I did.

Leftist!

A funny thing happened to me on the bus tonight. I was sitting near the driver who was an Arab. A bunch of Jewish teens were making a ruckus in the back of the bus and the driver asked them to lower the noise. They came to the front of the bus to "show the driver who's boss." I stood up between them and the driver and did not allow the teens to continue to harass him.

Frustrated and angry at me, they let loose their worst curse – "Leftist!" I should be ashamed of myself. I should remove my kippah because I am not a real Jew if I take an Arab's side against Jews.

I told them that actually I was a Rabbi Kahane supporter, but *derech eretz* (respect) comes before all. I doubt the punks ever heard of the great Jewish thinker.

I told the driver of their curse. I explained to him that I was actually the opposite of a Leftist, but "right is right" (no pun intended). He seemed to appreciate that.

We then had a short conversation about Arabs and Jews and the "conflict." He said we should all "just live together."

I said that it is difficult when most Israeli Arabs vote for parties that reject the very idea of the Jews to a right to their own country even though Israel benefits them so much.

He asked, "If all the Arabs would leave Israel, would there not then be war amongst the Jews? You need the Arabs to unite you."

He was being frank and I appreciated it.

I smiled. I am more than willing to see how that might work out. I was being frank as well.

A Worthy Night

I finally took part in a very worthy project that I was made aware of recently.

Last night, I did not sleep. I volunteered for the "Shomrim (watchmen) of Judea and Samaria." This organization was formed to help isolated Jewish shepherds secure their flocks from the ever-present danger of Arab thieves who sneak up at night. They are experts in stealing whole flocks in the wink of an eye; part of their culture and their expertise.

The loss of a flock that takes years to raise, destroys the lives of the owner and their families in a moment.

Besides the personal loss, it is yet another painful blow to the cause for which these idealists chose to live and shepherd there in the first place – to secure Eretz Yisrael for the Jewish people and prevent continuing Arab land grabs.

By Jews herding sheep in a wide area, Arabs cannot establish yet another illegal presence which the Israeli authorities are not quick to act on. The Arabs know this and so target these pioneers for nationalist reasons as well as booty. It's their contribution to Jihad.

Couples like the one who live in this isolated farm cannot work during the day and also guard at night. They must have help. The government is not their address.

Those who no longer have the strength to cope often give up and leave, delivering the very victory that the Arabs seek. These idealists are my heroes and so I decided it was the least I could do to give them a night.

The idea of "guard duty" is something that is familiar to anyone who has ever served even a week in the military. That was quite a few years ago for me and this was a deja vu experience. It made me feel old and young at the same time.

Older, because I am less tolerant of the ever-increasing cold that seeps through one's clothes and the feeling that the night seems to grow longer as the time goes by.

I felt younger as I looked up at the star-filled sky that

reminded me of my earlier guarding experiences. The silence of the night; distant sounds mingling with ones nearby brought back memories.

The comradery of a fellow guard and the time to exchange philosophy and rather personal history with a buddy is a unique experience. We sat adjacent to the pen which the sheep shared with some geese.

A donkey lay nearby and dogs diligently observed them all. I definitely learned some new things about the habits of these creatures that night. Between them and the stars above, I thought, how wonderful is the creation and its Creator.

The shepherd greeted us from his truck where he sleeps at night. Volunteers or no (volunteers are not available every night) he wanted to be close to his flock. He has heard too many stories about friends' lives wiped out in a single night.

I guess he was the type of man I expected to meet. A weathered look, few words, individualistic, rugged; we cannot do without these people if Israel is to prevail.

Just as the "West was won" with pioneers, and dreamers, so too is this small, holy piece of land that God has promised us won with believers and doers.

I don't know how much I really contributed that night, but it was a privilege I wanted to be part of.

A Shiva Call

I paid a shiva call this week; a particularly difficult one as I joined the "Women in Green" who organized a bus to take us to the village of Yitzhar in Samaria. There, we met Sofia and her little ones, aged one through seven. She is mourning her husband, Eviyatar Borovsky, the latest Jewish victim of Arab terror. The Israeli media was quick to point out that it has been almost a year and a half since the last "incident." Not to be too concerned. Jews will be knifed at bus stops from time to time. It happens – especially over there, in the "territories."

She is yet another very young widow left with five little ones. She is made to feel by many in the establishment that people like her and her family just get in the way of progress for normal Israel. Practical Israel understands how important it is to be accepted into the global village. Fanatic Jews that cling to ideas such as faith and national pride don't go over well. It looks so backward, even fanatical.

In her very crowded, small living room sat the deputy Minister of Defense, Danny Dannon on the worn sofa. He has a reputation as an outspoken patriot and thus was deemed the right one to represent the government on this sensitive occasion.

Sofia, clutching a photo of her family, including her late husband, implored the deputy minister to understand that Jewish blood is more important than Arab convenience. She explained that the Jewish residents of the area frequently begged the authorities not to remove security checks on the roads leading from known Arab terror centers to Jewish homes. These checkpoints save Jewish lives ... but they inconvenience Arabs.

It is of the utmost importance to the government that Israel is judged favorably abroad. The desire to be accepted is overwhelming. The rules of engagement for Israeli soldiers endanger Israeli soldiers on a regular basis.

When an Arab comes up to a military gate and steals, the guards may not use their weapon. Soldiers in the Negev are forbidden to travel on certain roads after dark for fear of local Bedouin rock attacks. Police vehicles in Jerusalem are pelted with stones at close range – and their only option is to flee. Indeed, a military judge recently called Arab attempted murder with stones "teenage rowdiness." This, after a father and baby were killed by such "rowdiness" on the Jerusalem-Hebron Road a year ago. Israel is still obsessed with being accepted.

Sofia and her neighbors live and breathe this 24/7. She explained how her children live in fear, how the local Arabs regularly come up to their village and initiate provocations as the Israeli security force watches for "unwarranted Jewish responses."

One of the residents explained to Mr. Dannon how he and his neighbors are forced to share the same bus stop with local Arabs and they must always be on the highest alert as they watch every movement of their fellow carefree Arab travelers. Is it Arab human rights or Jewish human life that should concern Israel? Something is wrong. Very wrong.

One cannot escape the feeling that the government does not and will not protect Sofia and her children from the fate of their husband and father.

Mr. Dannon just looked into Sofia's face and had no answers for her. No promise of a change in security policy, no security roadblocks or change of rules of engagement, just talk about how the government wants to build more in Samaria.

Has he consulted his boss, Netanyahu, who refuses to allow Jewish expansion in the "territories?"

The wounded terrorist who killed her husband is enjoying the best Israeli medical care, and after a lengthy trial and appeals, will reenter the terrorist "university and country club" – the Israeli jail. This terrorist has already spent four years in an Israeli prison and is now ready for his graduate program after which he has reason to expect another successful prisoner exchange (1000 for 1).

One may conclude from all this that Israel has a higher agenda than doing everything to prevent the spilling of Jewish blood.

Shall We Mourn?

Veteran PLO leader Saeb Erekat died of Coronavirus complications despite enjoying Israel's best medical care.

How many Jews were denied his hospital bed in this time of medical crisis I do not know. I do know that many Israelis are no longer with us due to the efforts of Mr. Erekat and company.

His death signaled a three-day period of mourning in the Palestine terror Authority and his face is seen on billboards throughout the PA, next to his mentor, the arch terrorist Yasser Arafat.

Israel / Jew haters' grief for Erekat is understandable. What is difficult to understand is the outpouring of grief and sense of loss of many Israeli Jews. They tell us he was against violence, a man of peace. He never personally killed a Jew.

Perhaps he did not kill any Jew with his hands as far as I know (I don't know his full biography as a terror member and leader). He was best known for libeling Israel and Jews, and encouraging others to kill them. He consistently heaped lavish praise on killers of Jews and fought to reward them and their families with generous payments. I think it is called "pay to slay."

He spoke of diplomacy that will lead to a "two-state solution with Jerusalem their capital" and "a just solution to the refugee problem" (flooding Israel with Jew-hating Arabs). Then the terror will stop. To the Left this was music and Erekat was the maestro.

Twenty-five years after the Oslo hoax most understand what that means – the end of Israel in an orgy of Jewish blood.

There does not exist a PLO map that includes a country called "Israel" with whom they say they want to live peacefully side by side.

The only ones being fooled are those that want to be, and so the Israeli Left pour out their hearts this day at the passing of a great friend of peace.

I don't seem to ever remember a similar outpouring of Leftist grief as Jews were murdered by Erekat's heroes. They are not interested in that grief. Weren't they "sacrifices of peace?"

What makes educated Jews so blind and so callous to their own people's suffering while idolizing our enemies?

I am still trying to understand.

4 / 2021

Jewish Values?

In the wake of the massive explosion of what is probably a major Hezbollah arms depot in Beirut port yesterday, Israelis debate the proper reaction towards the many civilian casualties.

In the wake of this accident, Israel has offered humanitarian aid and in solidarity, the Lebanese flag illuminated the entire city hall building in Tel Aviv. At this writing we have not yet seen public kaddish recited or candles lit for them. This outpouring of grief is reserved for select people – those in active conflict with Israel, as in the last Gaza confrontation.

Progressive, humanistic Jews are eager to send humanitarian aid to this enemy population. The enemy though, would rather die than be shamed by accepting aid from the hated Jews.

But the Jews never give up. They never stop yearning for love from their enemies. It's a Jewish thing. Progressives surely raise an eyebrow at the very notion of enemy populations?

What is the enemy population if not innocent civilians that have no quarrel or any particular feelings towards Jews? Only those who actually shoot at Jews that can perhaps be called the enemy. Even they might not really do so of their own free will.

The reality is that the Arab enemy population, brainwashed for generations to hate and kill Jews, is the same as the Jew-haters of the enemy population of Germany not long ago. Their cities were flattened by the enlightened Western allies just as Germany bombed them first. It was the war of light against darkness, good against evil. Whole societies were educated to eliminate the other.

Our Arab civilian neighbors have endless opportunities to show the tiniest hint of empathy when Jewish civilians in Israel are murdered by Arab terror.

Instead, they rush to show their satisfaction by sharing sweets at traffic corners and public squares (which they name after the mass killers of Jews).

Of course, our enlightened progressive brothers will wag

a moral finger and remind us that we are not like "them" (the condescending racism of lower expectations). What does that mean? Does it mean that we must train ourselves to weep when our enemies fall?

Wrong religion. King David frequently thanked God for the fall of his enemies, and they were not only males of fighting age.

Lebanon is an enemy country that is run by Hezbollah – dedicated to killing all Jews; not just in Israel, just as Germany was ruled by a popular anti-Semitic regime. They paid a price.

I don't recall Jews saying kaddish for German civilians; just as German civilians were not sorry about Jews their country murdered. Same with the Arabs. Does the Torah demand us to extend our love and mercy to the enemy population? A familiarity with the texts shows clearly that the answer is absolutely not.

So, do I shed a tear when my enemy falls? No, I read the Psalms of David that beseech God to destroy them and praise Him for just that. But then again what would David know about true Jewish values?

Seven Times Severe

Professor Ariel Porat is the president of Tel Aviv University. In a video he shared, Porat said, "Minds cannot tolerate a situation in which Jews in the State of Israel are scared to leave their homes ... out of fear for their well-being and property, but the attack on Arab citizens is an attack on those who are a minority among us, and is, therefore, seven times as severe."

Porat said, "More than any other people, we Jews need to understand the significance of attacking a person solely for their ethnicity or nationality." He said he was particularly shocked to see that the crowd of Israelis that had gathered to watch the brutal beating of an Arab driver in the Tel Aviv suburb of Bat Yam last week did nothing to stop the attack. "What a terrible sight," he said.

What a terrible sight indeed. The sensitive professor could not bear watching Jews attack an Arab in the midst of a wave of anti-Semitic, Arab pogroms that swept Israel.

Jewish violence? Nothing can be worse and nothing can upset a Jew such as the professor as much. He was visibly pained by the one case (played up by the Israeli press, of course) of an Arab attacked by a Jew; so much so that it trumped the pain of thousands of Jews that were assaulted (some killed) by Arab mobs during that bloody pogrom.

Our rabbis teach us, "When it really hurts, you yell." How many Jews would have to be killed in an Arab pogrom before the pain of his own people came before the pain of others.

"An attack on Arab citizens is an attack on those who are a minority among us, and is, therefore, seven times as severe."

I don't know his family tree but I would not be surprised if his parents and grandparents were among the founders of the state and actually once loved the land and people more than those who hate us.

It is a common phenomenon in Israel and in other Western countries.

I am not sure why self-hatred and the desire for national

suicide exists in the USA and other Western countries, but I believe I know what the root problem is in Israel.

Rabbi Kook hit the nail on the head a hundred years ago. He addressed the grandparents of people like Professor Porat and warned, "Your love of the land and people will not be shared by your children if you put Torah out of your lives."

One need not be a great sociologist to understand. Our roots are Torah. We are not a nation without it. Without strong roots, branches grow in strange directions and the fruits can be poisonous.

Useful Idiots

Over the many years of guiding there are a few individuals that I still vividly remember. I met a number of individuals who I still remember well. A few weeks ago I was recommended to a rather interesting person – let's call him Paul.

Paul has been blessed with long years in which he gained prominence in the publishing and literary world. He is urbane, cosmopolitan, educated, a proud atheist, and a Leftist. He is also Jewish.

I expected this to be a delicate and challenging assignment; the kind I enjoy. I like to educate and learn about all things Jewish and I thought this might be an opportunity for good intellectual conversation.

Paul chose to stay at the American Colony Hotel in East Jerusalem, popular with the pro-Arab journalist and literary crowd. This was the first time that I walked into that famous hotel as I met him that morning. It is not only not kosher, its staff do not speak Hebrew. After fifty years in Israel, still no Hebrew. One can say much without uttering a word.

Paul explained that he always stays there to express his "neutral" position on the "conflict."

Our adventure began as we got into a cab to be taken to the Mount of Olives with its amazing view of the city.

As we rode through the Arab neighborhood of Atur, I explained that Israelis are often pelted with stones here as I was once myself. "We are probably safer because we are in an Arab cab," I said.

Paul explained to his traveling partner (a non-Jewish secretary thirty years his junior) that terror has been an "element" in the "conflict" since the pre-state days as he mentioned the Irgun and Lechi as terror groups too.

I suggested that we must agree on the definition of terror before we draw parallels. The Jewish underground did not target kindergartens but rather British military and administrative targets like the Americans did to the British in 1776.

I also explained to his guest that the Arabs refused a number of compromise offers in favor of killing Jews.

At this point our driver entered the conversation. He turned and yelled at me, "You Jews are the terrorists. You kill children in Gaza! Also, you are not honest about the 1947 partition offer and Arab refusal."

The cab pulled up and as we left, Paul paid the driver and had a few words with him.

I asked, "What else did he have to say?"

Paul, in fact, told him that the Arabs rejected the compromise of 1947 and began a war.

"What did the driver say?"

"Could be."

So typical. Once they see that they can't lie to you, they shrug and say, well, maybe and change the subject.

We entered the Old City through the Lions Gate, which the paratroopers entered in 1967 when liberating the Old City.

Once inside the walls, I took our first left towards an entrance to the Temple Mount. As we neared, two policemen rushed up to us nervously and commanded us to back off.

Of course, I wasn't surprised. I've been there before. I innocently protested, "Why can't we enter the Mount?"

"Only Muslims allowed," insisted the cop.

I asked innocently as a tourist might, "but isn't there freedom of movement and prayer for all in Israel?"

He was not amused and became more nervous.

I asked, "Is this the apartheid I hear so much about?"

As we walked away Paul said to me, "You knew exactly what would happen didn't you?"

"Yes, I did and so did you, but your friend learned something that she would have otherwise never understood."

In one conversation he said that perhaps it would have been better if there were no Jewish state. I asked him why the Jews were the only people not deserving of a country. The Arabs have twenty-two. He did not respond to this. Then he warned, "You are losing the intellectual supporters of Israel in the US. You must stop with the settlements and provide a solution for the Palestinians."

I asked him, "Suppose a poll was taken today of Israelis and they were asked, 'if half a million Jews were expelled from their homes in the 'territories' and Israel gave everything to the Arabs except only Tel Aviv, would there be peace. What would they say? What would you say?' " He was not sure.

I added, "a great rabbi once said, 'I prefer an untolerated Israel to a tolerated Auschwitz.' "

Paul was proud to tell me how he and some of his literary friends used their influence with Israel to gain permission for a "Palestinian" to be allowed back into Jerusalem after being banned by the authorities.

I didn't know the reason for his banishment but he is back, thanks to Paul and friends.

The next morning, I saw him as Paul invited him to breakfast. I later learned that he wrote a book about the devastation Jews brought upon the world in history. Paul was intrigued with it and my guess is that he was promoting it.

I sat in the lobby waiting for Paul and his lady companion to join me for the tour. While I was waiting, I overheard a conversation between the man Paul was helping and another man, a European.

The author laughed as he explained how he used "the Jew" to get him back into the country. The word "Jew" did not sound any more endearing when spoken by the European. They both got a good laugh.

Poor Paul.

Poor silly Jews.

Poor useful idiots.

Compassion Is In Order

When Rabbi Yehudah Glick, religious freedom advocate and civil rights activist, was felled by four assassin's bullets, the country was shocked and outraged.

The Arab terrorist, a Jerusalem resident, first asked his victim, in perfect Hebrew, if he was indeed the civil rights activist, the one who had the nerve to advocate the right for all people, even Jews to pray on our holiest site, the Temple Mount. When answered in the affirmative, he let loose four bullets at point blank range.

The Arab terrorist was killed by the police in a shootout a short time afterwards. The terrorist's family and supporters praised the new "shahid" (martyr). Candies were distributed and loudspeakers from minarets sang his praise in his Jerusalem neighborhood. The children had yet another model to cheer and emulate.

Meanwhile, multitudes of Jews prayed for Yehudah Glick as doctors left little hope of recovery from his multiple wounds.

One of the more effective deterrents to terrorism is the destruction of the killer's home. This affects the family's "honor" and in that society "honor" is the reason to kill even family members. The home of the terrorist who pumped four bullets into Glick was slated for destruction as well. His family, advised by "peace" groups, appealed to the Israeli courts. They argued that it was unfair, collective punishment. They argued that Israel as a democracy should treat even or especially enemies with understanding and compassion. After all, Israel is the stronger of the sides and should exhibit magnanimity towards the weaker. So goes the Left philosophy.

The three judges presiding on the bench of Israel's Supreme Court decided in favor of the terrorist's family. They explained that Glick was recovering. No one was killed. Extreme measures were not called for. Compassion is in order.

The killer's family and supporters now have double reason for celebration.

There Was No Pogrom

It did not take long for the usual crowd to compare this week's butchery of four Jews as they stood in prayer with the Dr. Baruch Goldstein shootings in 1994. Every time a Jew is killed until today by an Arab, we are reminded by the Left how we are no better. What would they do without Dr. Baruch Goldstein?

They point out the "symmetry in the conflict." There is no bad side in this story, they explain. There is simply violence on both sides.

The peaceful wonderful men who prayed in Jerusalem threatened no one. Their only crime was being Jewish, like so many thousands of others murdered by Arabs in our land.

Oh, but remember Baruch Goldstein. There are two sides, say the Left.

One of the four this time was my younger cousin and father of six, Aryeh Kupinsky.

A few words about Dr. Goldstein:

I knew him and his parents. They were exceptional people and wonderful Jews who made Aliyah from New York.

Dr. Baruch Goldstein could have had a lucrative career in the USA as he was first in his class at Einstein Medical School. He chose to make his home in Hebron and serve as the regional physician there. He was adored by all.

Parents would take their children to his clinic – just to see his face. He often slept with his shoes on – just in case he had to respond to an emergency.

Treating a young woman with cancer, he told her, "I will do whatever I can for you as long as I can." He ended up sitting at her bedside reciting Psalms.

There was a bad car accident near Kiryat Arba involving an army jeep. At the scene, he saw a badly injured Ethiopian soldier and asked for his home phone number. When asked why, he said, "He is clearly a new immigrant and his parents will need emotional support."

There is a book full of these stories that the government has banned. It is called "Baruch Hagever" or "Baruch the Man".

Shortly before Purim, he treated his best friend and his son after being attacked by terrorists. They died in his arms.

Now we come to Purim and the day of the events. The army had warned Dr. Goldstein of coming trouble – a pogrom. He was asked to enlarge his emergency room and prepare for the worst.

He braced for the Arab onslaught, as Arab mosque loudspeakers and posters urged the population to "stock up on food and water and prepare for a curfew."

Curfews always follow a terror attack.

That evening he went to the Patriarch's tomb to hear the Purim Megillah. An unusual number of young Arabs were in the building chanting "slaughter the Jews!"

Why the army allowed them in is still unclear.

Witnesses saw him leaving the building as he could not hear the reading over the cries for Jewish blood, shaking his head saying, "I can't take it anymore."

The very same thing happened the next morning during the second reading.

He returned that afternoon in uniform (major) with his rifle and eliminated 28 of those screaming for Jewish blood. He was then bludgeoned to death by them.

His death was mourned as few are. His grave is still a site for pilgrimage (even though the government destroyed most of it) for his beloved community and beyond.

He was killed on Purim along with a number of the Arab mob that he took with him. There was no pogrom against the Jewish community on Purim. He made certain.

Some have suggested that because the government was under heavy criticism following the Oslo terror deluge, they felt the need to manipulate public opinion.

They had to paint the "Right" opposition in the worst possible colors as the real threat to Israel and not Arafat's killers who the government had armed.

The Goldstein incident, a calculated manipulation from the beginning, succeeded in deflecting public discontent – for a while.

I don't know if this theory is true. It would not surprise me.

Anything is possible in a period when government agent provocateurs infiltrated the "Right" to entrap and delegitimize them.

Yigal Amir, the assassin of Yitzchak Rabin, was incited to kill the prime minister by an agent named Avishai Raviv. He wasn't the only one sent on similar missions in that period as others were exposed as well. The government was desperate and all means were employed.

On a personal note, he was one of the physicians in the delivery room when my oldest son was born. I recall his smiling face as he shared an ice cream with me.

I have rarely met a more selfless, modest, dedicated Jew.

Who Wants Jerusalem?

I took an amazing tour this week with Aryeh King, member of the Jerusalem municipal council and founder of the "Israel Land Fund." He took us to the "frontiers of Jerusalem" – parts of our capital that most Jewish residents never see. It was eye-opening; alternately uplifting and disheartening.

We saw where brave Jews are pioneering a Jewish return to areas where our people have hitherto not ventured due to Arab occupation during Jordanian rule or Arab violence since. These brave young people are truly modern heroes in my eyes.

Aryeh is the foremost expert on the topic of Jerusalem's demographics, development and the politics that determine both. He has dedicated his public life to keeping Israel's capital as Jewish as possible.

It would seem that in the capital of the Jewish state along with "the most right-wing national government ever," his job would be superfluous. Think again.

Many on the "Right" and in the settlement movement have been frustrated with the pace of Jewish development in Judea and Samaria, including post '67 Jerusalem. (If there was unhindered permission to build as in "normal" parts of the country, the Jewish population there would double in five years, thus bringing down the cost of housing in Israel proper by 20% overnight.)

I learned case by case how "Mr. Freeze," as Aryeh calls the long-serving Prime minister Netanyahu, has been blocking Jewish development beyond the "Green Line." After hearing Netanyahu's great speech at the UN the other day and observing his success in foreign relations, it struck me that there is a strange dichotomy in this man. He is good on the "outside" but very problematic on the "inside."

The Jerusalem expert, Aryeh King, pointed out how Jerusalem's Jewish development has and is being thwarted by the government (Netanyahu) and the increasing Arab presence and development as clear policy directives from above.

To illustrate the problem, there are eight neighborhoods within the Jerusalem municipal boundaries that have big red signs at their entrance. These signs inform Jews that entering poses a danger of death and is illegal. This, in the eternal capital of the Jewish people. Talk about apartheid...

In these neighborhoods, you will not find an Israeli cop unless accompanied by military force. There, the things happen when there is no law enforcement or governance.

As unpleasant as these neighborhoods are to live in, they are highly popular places with tens of thousands of Arabs. Why? Because it is part of Jerusalem, which means access to employment, first-rate health care, welfare and humane treatment – things they do not enjoy under the "Palestinian" rule they fled.

Housing in these "Judenrein" Jerusalem neighborhoods is far cheaper than where Jews live. This is because there are hundreds of high risers going up illegally and thus inexpensively.

Result? Masses of Arabs make their way into these apartments and enjoy Jerusalem residency status and rights with very low housing costs. Their children attend Israeli public schools, the syllabus of which does not include gratitude to the welcoming Jews.

In some parts of Jerusalem, Arab neighborhoods like Sur Baher/Um Tuba have received permits for twenty-five thousand units, more than all of Jewish Jerusalem, spanning years! At the same time, there is very little construction permitted in Jewish areas, with most of it near the center of town where real estate is very expensive. This is driving young Jewish families out of the market and out of the city.

Any attempt to expand the Jewish presence in areas in or near Arab populated neighborhoods meet with an impenetrable wall of bureaucracy and political directives "from the highest levels." Far more Arabs are moving to Jerusalem in the areas of illegal cheap housing than Jews moving into the city. Price is everything.

Yes, this situation sounds absolutely counter-intuitive and you may ask exactly what we repeatedly asked Aryeh, "Why?"

Aryeh believes that Netanyahu sincerely does believe

in a "two-state solution." This he declared openly in his groundbreaking "Bar Ilan" speech. There he publicly parted ways with traditional Likud policy (it is still the official Likud platform). With this announcement, he joined the Left in their vision for the Land of Israel.

There is confusion by this sharp departure from Likud policy. Many believe that he really "didn't mean it," that he "has a plan." It is indeed confusing.

I said to Aryeh, "But Bibi constantly reminds the world that any area that Israel abandons becomes a launching pad for terror..."

"Yes, he does."

Charade

Arabbi from Tel Aviv-Jaffa was assaulted by a group of Arabs on the streets of Jaffa Sunday afternoon.

The victim, Rabbi Eliyahu Mali, has been identified as the dean of the local Hesder (pre-army preparatory) yeshiva, who was visiting property his yeshiva plans on purchasing from a local Jewish man.

While walking down a street in Jaffa, Rabbi Mali and Moshe Shendowitz, the director of the yeshiva, were attacked by a group of Arab assailants who surrounded the two and proceeded to harass and mock Rabbi Mali and Shendowitz.

When Rabbi Mali and Shendowitz took out their cellular phones to call for help, several of the Arabs assaulted them, punching and kicking the two victims. Shendowitz was injured in the attack, and was hospitalized afterwards.

Rabbi Mali filed a police complaint shortly after the assault. Roughly one hour after the complaint was filed, police managed to locate and apprehend two Arab suspects, Jaffa residents in their 30s.

"They punched and kicked me," said Shendowitz in an interview with Channel 13, emphasizing that the attack was nationalistically-motivated. "When people scream at you because you're wearing a kippah, that you're a 'settler' and that you should get out of there, that doesn't seem like a 'criminal' incident."

The above report that I just read has special significance for me. On Pesach, I led a group of visitors to that very yeshiva in Jaffa. We met the wonderful heroes on the front lines of the battle for Jewish communities in "changing" areas of our Jewish state. We heard about the wonderful work the yeshiva is doing for the Jewish poor of the "mixed" city of Jaffa. We learned how abandoned and empty synagogues are being revitalized both physically and spiritually.

Jewish life, almost snuffed out, is flickering again, but not everyone is happy about this. The Arabs and Left in Israel do not celebrate this return of Jewish life.

Arab residents, too, receive food packages and aid from the yeshiva's outreach program. The approach is, be a good and generous neighbor and the Arabs will accept the presence of Jews who contribute to the area.

When it was explained to me that the yeshiva offers this largesse and care to Arab residents as well, I felt a tinge of doubt. I doubt if one can really buy gratitude and friendship.

What and how much can material buy? Ask some Liberals and they will tell you that there is not a problem that cannot be solved with enough funding and empathy. Perhaps they personally have no beliefs or principles that transcend material incentive and don't consider the possibility that some people cannot be bought or appeased. Perhaps the truth about the enemies amongst us is not compatible with their world view and so they'd rather continue the charade?

The March Of Return

As Israelis nervously await the decision of Hamas to send or not send masses of Gazans to the border on a "march of return," I am reminded of the events that led to the creation of "Hamastan" and the fear and anxiety that has been a part of our lives since.

Before the abandonment of Gush Katif in Gaza in 2005, the government and press created an atmosphere for the mass expulsion of their fellow Jews. The public agreed to be lulled to sleep by the propaganda. They were oblivious to the pleas of their brothers and sisters about to have their lives ruined. They showed no empathy when thousands of men, women and children were dragged from their homes and wandered the roads of Israel as refugees. They felt secure and satisfied that the seductive lies of the leadership were true and just. The press and the powerful voices assured them all was just right.

The Left was about to fulfill a basic tenet of its ideology and much of the public were willing accessories, including the communities that lived just astride the Gaza border. "Land for peace" sounded right as long as it was other people's land.

I quote from an article written by Carolyn Glick in the Jerusalem Post in 2015. "The goal of the Left in destroying the Jewish communities (in 2005) and indeed the goal of the so called "peace movement" was laid out explicitly in November 2013 by Ron Pundak, Yossi Beilin's partner in creating the Oslo Accords with the PLO in 1993."

In an interview with the International Crisis group, Pundak explained, "Peace is not an objective by itself. It is a way to transition Israel from one era to another, to an era of what I consider is a normal state. 'Israelization' of society rather than 'Judaization'."

Demonization is a key component of the Left's campaign against Jewish Israel. In the withdrawal from Gaza and later the same on a much larger scale in Judea and Samaria, the public needed to become fully alienated from their fellow Jews whose lives were being shattered.

Respected opinion makers jumped on the anti-religious bandwagon and sought to outdo one another in stirring up hatred for the thousands of Jews in Gaza and their supporters.

Dan Margalit called for the institution of "numerus clausus" against religious Zionists serving in the military. "Strict limits," he said, "should be placed on the number of religious Israelis permitted to serve as officers."

Ari Shavit insisted that settlers deserved no protection from the IDF because as far as he was concerned, they weren't Israelis.

Yair Lapid wrote that the settlers were not his brothers, and he wouldn't have a problem going to war against them.

The media constantly drums into the public the message that "The settlers are our problem!" Just replace "settlers" for "Jews" and it sounds familiar in German.

The police, prosecution, and courts joined the crusade. Civil rights were trampled en masse. Pre-dawn raids arresting men, women and children and throwing them into ad hoc mass detention centers was the norm.

The Left was confident they were on the way to changing Israel forever. Just get rid of the last roadblock – the settlers and we are on our way to a non-Jewish Israel, a state of "all its citizens."

It was essential to weaponize the IDF and harness its respected name to do their dirty work. If the IDF cooperates, the public assumes it must be right.

The abandoned Jewish communities are now launching pads for Hamas's missiles that rain down on the same Jews who watched their brothers dragged from their homes with equanimity.

The communities bordering Gaza now fear tunnels popping up in their communities and must always be close to a bomb shelter. The residents are always armed and ready for a terror infiltration. Yes, life has changed since their neighbors are gone. They who heroically accepted the role of the first defense line for their neighbors and Israel are no more.

Will Hamas launch their promised mass "march home" into their homes? The Jews living around Gaza can find no rest.

Do they now understand that the Hamas "march of return" actually began in 2005 when their brothers and sisters were dragged from their homes and they just watched?

5 / 2021

A Great Army Is Not Enough

And so, another "round" seems to be drawing to an end. Number three of four since Sharon expelled thousands of Jews from Gaza and handed it to the enemy.

Our great leaders such as Rabin, Peres and Sharon assured us that there would be no rockets fired from Gaza once we left. Those who questioned were scoffed at as war mongers and fanatics and accused of causing the Israeli public to fear peace. They were wrong. Very wrong.

The Israeli public is battered and frustrated once again. We bury our dead; including old ladies and little tots, victims of rockets from Gaza.

Our leaders will tell us yet again that Hamas learned a hard lesson this "round" and will think twice before attacking Israel again. Do they all have the same speech writer?

The only thing Hamas thinks about is when to launch another "round." When a terror group fights a powerful army and state, victory is measured by surviving the contest. So far they are batting a thousand.

What was different about this "round?" Hamas surprised us with the number and sophistication of their missiles and range. Between "rounds" Israeli leaders basked in the calm and claimed credit. Meanwhile Hamas plans the next round. A preemptive attack on Hamas between "rounds" is not contemplated so as not to disturb the calm and not seem aggressive in the eyes of the world. We need the world to love us.

Nowhere in the world is there a situation even close to the madness here.

Israel is a top military power and Hamas is a (thanks to us, growing) terror group. Many thousands of rockets rain down on Israel from a small area run by some terrorists? Where did they get the stuff? How dare they! They hold Israeli prisoners in Gaza, and whole populations inside Israel are terrorized. And they expect to get another ceasefire in return for temporary quiet.

We continue to deliver humanitarian aid while they hold and torture our people. Who ever imagined that anything like this could ever happen? This can happen only to Jews who have lost their way. Nowhere else.

Since this is the land and people of the Tanach, we seek precedent in the Tanach. Saul was ordered by Samuel the prophet to totally destroy Amalek. Saul allowed his personal / political / humanistic considerations to get in the way of God's command. He spared the evil king. He told him that he was going to lose his throne because he had mercy on the wicked. Indeed, he ended up being wicked to the merciful.

Samuel assured him that "the eternity of Israel shall always endure" but Saul's career was over.

King Ahav of Israel defeated the Arameans and had mercy on their king. He not only let him live, but called him "my brother" and joined him in sacrificing to his gods.

When Hazael rebuilt his army, he attacked Israel and killed his "brother" Ahav.

Our enemies today must have read the Bible. A country cannot allow for a situation where its people live in constant fear, especially one that rose from the ashes of the Holocaust.

Having a great army is not enough.

A Lonely Death

The Israel Prison Service announced that Hamas security prisoner Bassam a-Sheikh died of cancer early Sunday at Assaf HaRofeh Medical Center. The prisoner, age 46, was terminally ill and was hospitalized for some time. He was imprisoned in Israel since 2015 for murder, attempted murder, kidnapping, coercion, false imprisonment, membership in a terror organization and contact with the enemy. That was the press announcement.

Specifically, the deceased cancer patient brutally murdered Rabbi Henkin and his wife in front of their children. The children were spared because the killer's weapon jammed.

The passing of this monster attracted attention and the father of another terror victim forced the prison authorities to share information under the Freedom of Information Act. He discovered the five-star conditions that terrorist murderers enjoy in Israeli jails. He found out specifically that the murderer of Rabbi and Mrs. Henkin received medications for his cancer treatment that are denied to Israeli citizens.

I will explain: In Israel, there is what is referred to as "a basket of medicines," which means that there are some very expensive medicines that are "not in the basket" and are not provided by "the national health system." Israelis who need them must find a way to personally finance them.

In Israeli prisons, Arab murderers receive every medicine and treatment, no matter the cost, unlike Israeli citizens.

Of course, the Palestinian Authority accuses Israel of purposely killing the "martyr" and terrorist revenge will follow. I am not surprised at the PA terror authority that our government created in 1993 (Oslo Accords).

Unlike those who know so much more than us plain citizens, I never believed that we could buy our enemies' acceptance, let alone their love.

A prominent leader of the extreme Left Meretz party, Mr. Mossi Raz, expressed his feelings about the death of this terrorist.

He bemoaned the "lonely death of a man who died without family or emotional support in a prison cell."

Do I recall him getting so choked up over the Henkin family?

Which is our bigger problem, the wild dogs circling us, or the ones who coddle them? I know the answer.

Just A Slap

Does it really matter if a "Palestinian" girl smacks an Israeli soldier across his face? Turning the other cheek is a classic Jewish ideal, isn't it? In today's Israel one might think it is.

So what if she spit in his face?

So what if she kicked him and hit him repeatedly?

So what if she repeatedly cursed the soldier?

So what if an Israeli soldier (someone's son or father) quietly absorbed the humiliation as the cameras recorded the shame for the world to see?

"Sticks and stones can break my bones..."

Israel is debating this latest "incident." Voices of "reason and temperance" praise the "restraint" shown by the soldier. These are the same voices that thought it was a wonderful idea to bring arch terrorist Arafat to our land with the ensuing Oslo bloodbath.

They applauded the retreat from South Lebanon (into which the Hezbollah terror army immediately entered and butchered our SLA allies who we abandoned).

These are the voices who cheered the expulsion of thousands of Jews from Gush Katif and northern Samaria and helped create "Hamastan" with its torrent of rockets and death tunnels.

How many times were we assured by those "who know" that the above will make the world love us and bring peace? The same experts applaud the behavior of the humiliated soldier, representing a "rational" Israel, an Israel that the world will love. There was a time when such a humiliating scene was inconceivable. What does this do for the morale of the country?

Something has changed. Some of us have tired, before our enemies have. Some of us have lost the strength to endure.

As former prime minister Ehud Olmert, who offered unprecedented concessions to the enemy, said, "We are tired of fighting..."

The same tired voices urged Israel to give the Golan Heights to Assad in return for the dream of "eating hummus with our new friends in Damascus."

Why are we so love starved? Why are we so willing to humiliate ourselves? Two thousand years of being humiliated and scorned may have something to do with it. Having our own country, strong and free, was supposed to finally change this. For many, it has not.

There are those who would rather be spat upon than be accused by the "world" of unacceptable behavior, and so the humiliated soldier was following the rules of the starved for love and acceptance.

Please Don't Save Me

Have you seen the demonstrations by Blacks in solidarity with their Jewish neighbors, victims of anti-Semitic murders by Blacks recently? You didn't? Neither did I. And you will not see it, but what did we see? We saw Jews march in the heart of Brooklyn behind a BLM (Black Lives Matter) leader. They expressed solidarity with Blacks killed by (non-Jewish) police, even as Jewish property was vandalized by rioting Blacks, and Jews attacked for being Jews.

It's a uniquely Jewish thing to want to be accepted by their tormentors. Jews led the civil rights movement in the sixties and idealistic Jews were killed for the cause. It's not new.

Directly following the civil rights movement then led by Jews, there was an explosion of Black anti-Semitism as the siege of Jewish inner-city neighborhoods began. Those Jews who could, fled the menace. Others cowered in fear.

In the seventies, I lived in an inner city neighborhood in Brooklyn. There, my grandfather was almost killed by "urban youth" because he could not deliver some change on his way to shul on Friday night. We lived in fear. Not once did a Jew attack a Black person, young or old.

At that time, I worked for a travel company. My job was to encourage churches to visit Israel. I would speak to clergy – often in their communities.

I was invited to a Black church in Harlem. It did not take long before I realized that the trek from Brooklyn was in vain. The pastor lectured me, saying that he would never lead his church to Israel because it was a racist country. He complained that Israel did not accept the "Black Hebrews" (a cult from Chicago) as Jews. He proceeded to get other things about Jews off his chest.

I asked him from where does anti-Semitism originate in the Black community? After all, Jews led the civil rights struggle and paid a heavy price for it.

He snorted, "Jews simply use the Black community for

political and economic gain. Jews are selfish and conniving." (He was kind enough not to accuse me of killing their god.)

The long trip from Brooklyn was not in vain. I learned important things.

Why are Poles, Italians, Irish and other ethnic communities not subject to Black hate and violence as are the Jews? It finally hit me. It is because they never tried to save them or anyone else. (It might also have something to do with the fact that the Jews are least likely to own a firearm.) Other communities simply mind their own business. They don't insist on saving anyone. Most communities place their own interests first. People don't like to feel beholden.

Jews are surprised when their best efforts to help are unappreciated and then scorned. This is one of the tragedies and ironies of Jewish life in the Exile.

A rabbi once wondered aloud, "Why does that person dislike me? I never tried to help him?"

The Last 20%

I just returned from a visit to the US, a place I once called home. It is always an experience of mixed emotions and observations.

I was happy to find that the best deli in the world is still alive and well in Brooklyn. Same is true for smoked and pickled fish. The shopping is great and there was a minyan or a Torah class on demand. The Orthodox community that I stayed with is doing very well.

I spent one weekend in the lovely "Hamptons" and another where my favorite boyhood memories lay – the "Catskills." Truly beautiful places. I appreciate those never-ending mountains and lakes even more than Brooklyn corned beef – I think.

This trip, I did not experience or observe any anti-Semitism. During my previous visit, I was shocked when someone on a supermarket line began ranting about "you people who think you control the city..." I felt certain then that if one person yells it, there are others in hearing range who agree. My hosts thought I was paranoid.

I did not experience anything like that this time. On the contrary, people were rather nice. Jews are doing well financially. The Orthodox live in robust and supportive communities and increasingly are united politically (Conservative, firmly pro-Israel...).

Is my conclusion then that life has never been better for American Jewry in 2015? As one who chose Israel over the US many years ago, my conclusions may be somewhat prejudiced, but I try to be a student of history and seek the bigger picture.

I remember telling myself and others that one major reason for making Aliyah was to be certain that my grandchildren would marry Jewish. The trend was clear in the seventies and the curve on the graph has been rising.

Most studies tell us that there are between five and six million Jews in the US today, less than 2% of the population. When I was a lad, we were told we were six million strong, a very influential

3% of the population. Then, we were the powerful big brother to little Israel of only about two million embattled Jews.

Since then, the general US population has grown greatly while Jews (non-Orthodox) have the lowest birth rates in the country. Assimilation (among non-Orthodox Jews) has reached over 70%.

If these trends don't take an unexpected turn, the Jewish population will fall to one million within a couple of generations – most of them Orthodox. At that point, there could be thirty million Muslim Americans.

AIPAC, ADL etc., if they still exist, shall be poor competitors for their Muslim counterparts. US politicians will know which dinners they need to attend.

University students, who are now exposed to relentless anti-Israel and anti-Semitic campaigns on campuses, will be the ones running the country in twenty years. It will be difficult, or impossible, to reverse their "anti" views of Jews and Israel.

There will be a point when the remaining Jews who have not yet totally assimilated will begin to feel isolated. It is then that they will consider Jerusalem as more than just a yearly Passover promise.

Our sages tell us that 80% percent of Jews chose to remain in the "fleshpots" of Egypt and they disappeared. The remaining 20% were rushed out before their bread had a chance to rise.

Our rabbis teach us that "the actions of the fathers are a sign for the sons."

How will the remaining 20% leave?

2/2021

From Where The Hate?

An interesting thing happened to me in my local pharmacy today. First some background:

The staff of the pharmacy are Arabs. We have a good rapport and we even converse in Arabic (they kindly help me when necessary).

We actually enjoy a mutually beneficial relationship as I bring coins for them to change into paper bills. I have access to these coins from a charity box (pushka) that I use to collect charity in my synagogue.

The organization that I volunteer for, "Honenu", provides free legal aid to Jews; civilians and military who find themselves challenged by the legal system as a result of "nationalist controversy" i.e., with Arabs. Honenu also supports the families of Arab terror victims and demands strict enforcement of the law against the perpetrators.

They play a unique role in Israel today that tends to be especially punishing to Jews who stand up to Arab nationalist assault. The Left label their work as political and "Right" wing. They don't like them.

My philanthropic activity in shul has allowed me some very interesting observations about my fellow congregants and perhaps about Israeli society today.

I have my "steady customers" who thank me for the opportunity to contribute. I have my sometime and never "customers." And then I have my "never ever with a vengeance customers".

The latter are the openly ideological opponents to what they see as a "Right wing cause." I get complaints, insults, arguments, attempts at shaming – you name it. They cannot look at me in or out of shul. I am a non-person.

I have made another interesting observation.

The hard-core Leftist opposition to my activity is mostly from England. Why would that be?

It may have something to do with either English education/ culture, or Jewish life there, or the meeting of the two. It would be an interesting study.

Let us return to the pharmacy. When I entered this morning, one of the more vocal opponents to my activity was there too. I greeted the staff in Arabic and emptied my pushka onto the counter. His body language expressed his feelings. He left and then returned a few minutes later.

He just had to warn the Arabs about me. Raising his voice, he pointed a finger at my pushka and asked them, "do you know what his organization is! Look it up! Do you know who you are helping!"

They were surprised by his outburst, but not particularly interested. He left in an angry huff. The Arabs and I had a cordial parting.

I would love to know, Mr. Leftist, from where does this hate of yours come?

Why The Fuss?

Israel's foreign minister and head of the "Yesh Atid " party said the following at an international forum on anti-Semitism:

"The anti-Semites weren't only in the Budapest Ghetto. The anti-Semites were also slave traders who threw people bound together with chains into the sea. The anti-Semites were the extremist Hutu in Rwanda who massacred Tutsis. The anti-Semites are Muslim fanatics who have murdered millions of other Muslims in the past century. The anti-Semites are ISIS and Boko Haram. The anti-Semites are people who beat LGBT people to death. The anti-Semites are those who hunt people not because of what they did, but because of who they are. Because of how they were born."

Mr. Lapid, did you know that before and after the slave trade, Hutus, ISIS and any other form of hatred there was and is hatred of the Jewish people.

It is the most unique form of hatred in history. It is not limited to place or time or circumstance. Anti-Semites come in all forms, all ideologies and in all places. One should not equate in the same breath other wrongs with those perpetrated against the Jews. Our enemies constantly try to destroy or minimize the memory of Jewish suffering. If anti-Semitism is everything, then it is nothing.

If I misunderstood you, Mr. Foreign Minister, I am certain that many others have as well. I thought you might understand that.

The Torah bestows upon the people of Israel what may seem like a strange blessing, "Israel is to be a nation that shall dwell alone and not be influenced by the other nations."

In its wisdom, the Torah tells us that the nation of Israel cannot fulfill its divine mission of leading humanity to a better place if it is influenced by that imperfect world and loses its unique character and values.

The struggle to remain a Jewish nation, not influenced by the nations of the world, is in effect Jewish history.

Paganism, Hellenism, Christianity, Islam, Communism, Integration; all had their appeal in their time. Not all members of the Jewish nation withstood those temptations. They abandoned Jewish history.

Our foreign minister, in his speech, crossed a red line. He explained to the world in the name of the Jewish state that we are no different. We are not unique. Our history is not unique. Jewish pain and prejudice are exactly like that of any other nation. He was assuring the nations that the unique hatred of Jews is something we would not dwell upon if that would please them and help us to enter the family of nations. The foreign minister created another precedent as Israel's number one spokesman to the nations. Upon entering office, he ordered the "gay flag" hoisted next to Israel's flag outside the building. If one wondered what does the Jewish nation stand for in essence? That was his answer.

The Jewish nation not only does not dwell alone. We can be as un-Jewish as the rest; even more so. This is the message of the Left in Israel. Is there nothing special about the Jewish state?

As former Prime Minister Olmert said, "I want a country that is fun to live in." Those who want a "nation of all its citizens" will have to explain that the Judaism of four thousand years is mistaken. That wasn't authentic Judaism. The nations of the world may ask themselves, "what was the reason for establishing this Jewish state; a place to have fun?"

What was the Balfour Declaration all about? What did we vote for in the UN? Why destabilize an entire region with the return to a land that is not special for a people who are not special. If it was just about physical security, why did it have to be exactly where there is opposition? What was the historic need and justification? Why all the fuss?

My Arabic Tutor

The following is an interesting glimpse into the mindset of Arabs in Israel. For a few months now, I have been learning Arabic with a private tutor. She responded to an ad I placed at the Israeli university in which she studies social work and also has a job at a well-known communications company. She knows Arabic, Hebrew and English and we have had a good rapport.

The following is our last communication via WhatsApp. I quote word for word including her sometimes less than perfect English:

She: How are you?

Me: Good, but I am distressed by the violence.

She: Me too. I hope it will end soon.

Me: Do you have any insights about the problem of violence within Arab society? Do you know if it is so in other Arab countries?

She: I don't think so because in other Arab countries there is a government that stands to protect the Arab, but unfortunately in Israel, they are always against it even if they're right. The violence in Arab society came as a response to all the repression that the police and the Zionists. In Sheik Jarrah they take their homes without any special reason to.

Me: I see that we have lots to talk about if we are to understand each other. I follow events very closely and keep a diary for over thirty years. The facts about the conflict don't escape me. Many people are brainwashed and don't want to learn facts. They are comfortable with their narrative. What is the real reason why Arabs harm Arabs so often? Where I live, I don't often see police yet we don't harm and kill each other.

She: You are asking a very wide question and I can't give you a full answer. Listening or reading facts are nothing like living them. As an Arabic Muslim girl who lived here since forever, I can assure you this state (sic) situation has nothing to do with Arab violence, but more of its policies violence and apartheid system.

And I totally understand your point of view since you are Jewish and want to protect your people but the only fact that I see is that no one in this country gives us minimalist rights. If it's to pretend or even to live(?). I feel so sorry for the people in Gaza, the children who lost their parents and to the people in Sheik Jarrah being arrested, killed and beaten to go away from their own home.

Me: Let me tell you a story about when I was a rookie tour guide. I was guiding on a bus with a driver named Ahmed. As we passed Tzipori, he said, "today there are Jews who live where my family lived until the Zionists threw us out in 1948."

I asked him where he lives today.

He said, "Nazareth."

I asked him if he had a house, a good job, schooling and health care for his children?

"Yes," he said.

I said, "if your side would have won the war, we Jews would not have a house, job, school or health care. We would all be dead."

"Achmad," I told him, "be thankful."

She: I'm sorry but I have to say that this is so rude Shalom! You can't steal a whole life from somebody, his childhood, his everything and after so many years this someone finally has a home and family and he has to say thank you!? Do you think getting another home is easy? Do you think that being immigrated(sic) is a simple thing or what...? Are YOU ready to thank someone who stole your home because you got another home and job after that?

Me: No one stole his home. Tzipori was a hostile village used to attack and kill Jews. There were battles and people were dislocated.

The Arabs started the battles. The Jews did not want it. The Arabs tried to kill all the Jews, as they said they would. They tried and failed. Instead of kicking him out of the country or killing him, although he was the enemy, he was allowed to stay and prosper.

Ten million Germans were kicked out of their homes after the war. They don't complain or carry out acts of terror and revenge against their former countries, they understand that they launched a war, they lost and there is a price. They are glad to be alive.

She: You think that the Arabs are frustrated though they have a beautiful life in a perfect country to live in. So let me tell you how it looks. You just look from one side. Thanks to the whole world that is looking now from the Palestinian side, they are seeing that this perfect country is not as perfect as it seems. I don't mean the way it looks but in the way it looks at the Arabs like we are the enemy. We didn't start everything in 1947-8. Most of the Arabs migrated from their land and that's how we got to be two sides. Palestinians and Zionists.

Me: Actually, the Arabs did start everything in 1947-48. If you know the history, you know that. The Jews tried everything to prevent the bloodshed. They agreed to every compromise but the Arabs said no way. The history is very clear. It's very easy to access the facts. Had the Arabs won that war as they declared, we Jews would all be dead. That is the difference. The Arabs that stayed became citizens. They are the only free citizens in the Mid-East. They can work and study freely, like you. No one bothers you I assume. What exactly are you deprived of? What is your complaint? I don't understand.

She: In 1947-48 the Arabs were forced to leave their homes. I don't have to say thank you for working and studying. The country did not do it for me. I worked for it. And besides, I am concerned for other Arabs who are not as fortunate as me and live-in conditions where they are not respected. You don't have to only rely upon the history that you know. Look at what is happening today. Arabs are being forced out of their homes in Sheik Jarrah. The whole world stands with the Arabs in Sheik Jarrah because that is the truth.

Me: The fact that the whole world says one thing doesn't mean it is correct. The whole world stood by while they killed six million Jews and did nothing about it. That doesn't mean that it was right. In 1947-48 it was the Arabs who decided to kill all the Jews. Thankfully they failed. Some Arabs fled their homes in fear, some were told by their leaders to leave and return to take Jewish property after the Arab armies killed all the Jews, some were expelled by Israeli forces.

As far as Sheik Jarrah goes, Jews bought that land and lived in the homes for decades before they were kicked out by Jordan in 1948. Their homes were then given to Arabs by Jordan. After 1967, the Jews demanded their homes be returned to them. After a very long legal process they are finally able to return and the illegal residents must now finally leave.

She: I can see that a huge part of this narrative is wrong and let's say it is true, no one is given the right to kill poor people and to protect others just for their religion. You lived so many years thinking that it's the fault of the Arabs and I'll not convince you of another, because you'll not be convinced.

(She then sent me a quote from Noam Chomsky proving that Israel is the moral criminal in the conflict.)

Me: I am open to learning and hearing facts that I am not aware of. I am not an expert in many things but in this I am well versed and always ready to hear other opinions as long as it is based on fact. (She may have thought that Professor Chomsky was just an honest Jewish thinker who tells it like it is.)

Me: I am very aware of Noam Chomsky and that he is the most notorious anti-Israel self-hater. He is very famous for this.

I am aware of it all and I know the truth. I fear that you have not looked wide enough. You speak in slogans and cartoons. That is not fact or history. Why don't you ask the professors at school? They may teach you facts that you can trust.

She: This is fact and this is history. If you are not convinced you can see all the events that are happening this last week because Palestinians are being killed for just protecting another. Listen, I just don't want to continue this conversation for one reason. It is because you lived so many years and you are convinced of these facts and can't change it in a one-hour conversation. You will always stand with your people and so will I. I prefer not to continue this conversation because we are not arriving at a point.

Me: Yes, I have encountered this many times. It is very sad, actually very scary. For me, this conversation was revealing, or rather confirming what I already knew. The Israeli Arabs, no matter how good their lives are in Israel they will be antagonistic to it.

Just A Symptom

For as long as Jews yearned to return to the homeland and, as reflected in the Zionist movement, the aim was to have a Jewish state in Eretz Yisrael with as many Jews and as few non-Jews as possible. The idea was to create a country and environment dominated by Jews and Jewish culture who would be solely responsible for its destiny. To that end, the Zionist movement from the outset dedicated itself to purchasing land and bringing Jews to settle it.

The return to Zion was not a cosmopolitan movement. It was not a call to humanity to come to Eretz Yisrael, join hands and create a new multi-cultural society. It was not planned to be a state of "all its citizens." It was a uniquely a Jewish idea.

A good portion of the Arabs of Eretz Yisrael were attracted there by the development and employment opportunities that the Jews brought with them. Before the arrival of the Zionist, the land was famously desolate.

The Arabs that the Jews met upon arrival were relatively few in number and lived in squalor. The Jews offered the Arabs cooperation and prosperity (the influential Socialist element of the Zionist movement believed that class affiliation would overcome national / religious tension) but from the onset the Arabs refused the hand offered. The history is well known.

Bottom line, after the 1948 invasion of tiny, just born Israel by the Arab world, many local Arabs left the war-torn areas. Some, the smart ones, stayed and though former enemies, were granted Israeli citizenship.

This did not mean that the Arabs who remained were happy that they lost the war or embraced the victors. It also did not mean that Israel would not have been happy if all the Arabs left. This sensitive subject was not discussed in polite company.

When the yearly demographic statistics are published, the item of greatest concern is – how many Arabs to Jews? How many babies per mother? Going up or down? Jewish immigration numbers. Where is the next wave of Jewish immigrants going to come from?

Is the Galilee majority really Arab? Oy! What can be done? This existential concern is kept under the carpet, but discussed in earnest by Israeli policy makers.

I recall in the 1980s, Ariel Sharon, then housing minister in the Begin government, launched a massive campaign of "Judaizing the Galilee." This included creating infrastructure and incentives for Jews to move to parts of the Galilee that were "threatened" with Arab demographic domination. It won wide support and was lauded as the classic Zionist endeavor at the time.

I wondered then, how do Arab Israelis feel about this? How does it feel to have your very presence considered a threat to the country in which you are a citizen? They must have resented it on some level.

Arabs did not complain much about it then. Times were different. The facade of coexistence on Israel's terms was still strong.

This morning I heard an Arab Knesset member explain the countrywide Arab pogroms against their Jewish neighbors. She said that it is insulting that groups of Jews buy Arab property in "mixed" cities in order to "Judaize" it.

She referred to the young idealistic families organized into "Torah nuclei" to bolster and revitalize weak and declining Jewish populations in what were once Jewish neighborhoods. Increasingly, emboldened Arab crime and anti-Semitism have been chasing large numbers of Jews from their homes.

Not all Jews can leave. They are stuck and suffer hostility and attacks from Arabs in their building, street and neighborhood.

The Arab MK claimed that "Judaizing" these areas is a racist policy and is the reason that Arabs pour their wrath upon Jews.

During the nationwide pogrom, Arabs attacked in areas where there were no "Judaizing" efforts under way. To this the MK responded there is "frustration" with the situation in the Temple Mount and Gaza.

In recent years the courts have for the first time instructed that Arabs be permitted to purchase homes in Jewish towns on land that was purchased by the Jewish National Fund for specifically Jewish settlement to strengthen the Jewish nature of the country. (Jews rarely venture into Arab villages and towns, let alone buy homes there.)

There was no shame about the goal or the means of ensuring the greatest Jewish presence possible in all parts of the Jewish state. It was natural. This was Zionism. Today this is a subject that elicits guilt and shame in some Jews. What has changed?

Yes, to be an Arab minority in the Jewish country that you fought against, and lost, is not easy from a psychological perspective. From a practical perspective, being a citizen of the Jewish state is heaven, but "man does not live by bread alone." I get it.

For some Israelis, guilt in winning the War of Independence and the subsequent Arab flight has blinded them to the severity of the recent countrywide Arab onslaught in Israel. They seek reasons, root causes, symmetry.

The Left "mea culpa" chorus makes excuses for violence against Jews. These same guilt-ridden Jews pounce on the unusual case of a Jew attacking an Arab. This, more than massive assaults on Jews, is intolerable in a Jewish state.

Arabs try to solve their identity problem by remaking the Jewish country to one of "all its citizens." The next stage should be clear.

Tens of torched synagogues during the pogroms reflect their ultimate goal.

Arabs in Israel have Leftist allies who also don't want a Jewish country, but a country of "all its citizens." They don't understand that the next stage of "liberation" does not include them.

So, there it is. We have two problems: One is the Israeli Arab who will never accept Jewish sovereignty in return for material gain and human rights. The other and more serious one is that there are Jews who don't want a Jewish country, and ally with frustrated Jew haters. The Arabs are encouraged by these Jews.

Once Jews are strong in their identity and purpose, the rest will fall into place.

The Arab problem will be diminished as their current rising expectations will be thwarted. This prospect may cause some of them to consider leaving the Jewish state. We should assist them. It should be a major goal of the country.

The Left have been doing their best to turn Jews away from Jewish identity and sense of rightness. They want to dejudaize the Jews. There is a Kulturkampf for the soul of the Jew in Israel today.

This is the root problem. The Arabs are just a symptom.

Irreconcilable

I watched an interesting discussion today. Alex Tselten was raised in the former USSR and has a high-tech career in Israel. He has a keen interest in all things related to Israel. I would describe him as a Right-wing patriot and very secular, similar to many that made Aliyah from the USSR. He produces and hosts a very interesting program online called "meet the professors," where he interviews Israeli intellectuals from the social sciences and humanities.

Today, he interviewed Dr. Abed Hasab, a Muslim intellectual who is well integrated in Israel's academia. He is an atheist and was one of the leading figures in the Israel Communist party with many Israeli Arabs and some Jews.

Dr. Hasab describes himself as an Arab, Israeli and a Palestinian. His background and social position are not typical of most Israeli Arabs. He has spent his life giving thought to his own identity and engaging in the politics that emerge from it.

He says he is a proud Israeli because of the opportunities allotted to him and his family in the Jewish state. He denounces the corruption of the Arab world, including the "Palestinian Authority."

He decries Jewish "settlements" in the "territories" because they block a viable Palestinian state and a "two state solution."

He acknowledges that Israeli Arabs will never want to leave Israel for an independent Palestinian state and that, in fact, many in the PA would happily trade their Palestinian citizenship to become Israeli citizens.

Yet he believes there should be a Palestinian state. Perhaps after that, there can be one "state of all its citizens" including everybody. (That, of course, won't be a Jewish state.)

He is definitely against Israeli Arabs serving in the Israel army and taking up arms against "brother Arabs" as he puts it.

He is for integration of Jews and Arabs in education and beyond.

Alex tried to make sense of some of the apparent contradictory sentiments of the Arab intellectual. Clearly, Dr. Hasab has sharp contradictory feelings. I fully understand them.

I believe he and many other Arab Israelis will never feel totally at home in the Jewish country that affords them so much opportunity. This atheist intellectual acknowledges his good fortune to live in the Jewish state, but cannot imagine defending it from its enemies. This reflects deep seated tribal, ethnic and cultural moorings.

All this is not new to me. They were not Zionistic in 1948 when they tried to kill their Jewish neighbors, and they have internalized that defeat. The Arab population generally votes for Arab Knesset members who are fiercely anti-Zionist.

I understand their frustration and mixed feelings about living in the Jewish state despite, or perhaps because of, how beneficial it is to live here. They have a problem.

What I found to be more interesting is that Alex could not make sense of the contradictions.

He pointed out that many people fought each other for a long time and today they are at peace such as his former country and Germany. Today they are friends. Why can't the Arabs (PA) leave their narrative of Israel hatred and understand the practical benefits of merging with Israel as Israeli citizens and willingly identify with it and defend it?

He explained that in the USSR all Soviet citizens served in the army including Muslims and Jews. Clearly Alex does not feel the deep emotional roots, identity and culture of the Arabs.

Muslims are taught that their religion displaced a false and evil one and that Jews are meant to be ruled by Muslims. Arabs find it very difficult to forgive Jews for defeating and thus humiliating them. Arabs are taught in the Koran and by their long historical experience, that Jews just don't beat Arabs.

Not acceptable.

Alex is the product of a Soviet materialist culture where emotion is discouraged. Historic memory and religious loyalty (except for the Communist state, of course) were repressed.

Alex has that rare combination of Israeli patriotism but complete distance from Judaism and religious belief.

The early secular Zionists (fast becoming "post-Zionists") also had no use for Judaism or Jewish religious faith. Over a century ago, they hoped to convince the Arabs of the benefits of building a new Socialist society together with them. Together, they would eliminate hatred and backwardness.

They were disappointed when they were forced to fight the Arabs who did not share their progressive ideas. Alex seems to be dreaming the same dream as the atheist Zionists did a hundred years ago.

The Jewish idealists of over a century ago have long abandoned their dreams and now lead the "peace camp" that longs to give away the land their fathers loved for some quiet and a "normal life."

Alex still loves his secular Israel and has not yet lost his dream of convincing the primitive Arabs to see the light.

How long will it take for him to understand what Dr. Hasab was saying?

The Last Ones Standing

The small "National Religious" party faces opposition from every corner of Israel's political spectrum. From the Left, for the traditional political / religious reasons; From the Arabs, the same. From the Haredim for being Zionists and daring to express their politics in spiritual / Jewish terms: Only they represent true Torah / Jewish values. Any other claim is either childish or renegade. There is yet another critic. The traditional "Right." The Likud is terribly upset with the little "National Religious" party these days. If for the Haredi parties, budgets for their community and institutions are most important, for the Likud it is "being in power."

Power for power's sake is everything. Why do I say this?

Netanyahu recently slaughtered yet another sacred cow (previously he voted for the expulsion of thousands of Jews from their homes in Gush Katif; he declared his support for a "Palestinian" state, and more) when for the first time he invited the anti-Zionist Muslim Brotherhood party to share power.

Members of the "Ram" Islamic party are dedicated terrorist supporters, for which they make no excuse.

The "National Religious" party said that they would not be a part of this outrage. They warned that if this red line was crossed, the Jewish state would have lost its moral foundation.

For the Likud, turning down a chance for power is treason.

Likud supporters accuse, "by insisting on your silly principles, the Left will form a government and the 'Right' will lose power."

Why is power necessary? Is there an ideology that warrants that power or is it all about political patronage and power for power's sake? Is everything for sale in the quest for power?

Today's Likud party is the heir of the historic "Herut" of Menachem Begin, which in turn was the political movement founded by Ze'ev Jabotinsky. It has come a long way. What was once an uncompromising fighter for the land of Israel and Jewish pride has become the equivalent of a soccer team with passionate fans. Winning is the thing, the only thing. Whoever gets in the way of a shot at the championship is the enemy of the club.

The Religious Zionists see the politics of the Jewish state as something much more serious than winning an election – something actually holy.

Rabbis Alkalai, Kalischer, Mohliver, Reines, Kook and Maimon were some of the prominent leaders of the Religious Zionist movement from as early as the mid-nineteenth century. They understood that without a soul, a body is meaningless and cannot survive. They were inspired not by European political thinkers or by Karl Marx.

When Rabbi Kook was chief rabbi of pre-state Palestine, the Zionist movement was dominated by the Socialist, anti-religious camp. Jewish labor, farming, defense of the land and eventually statehood were both the means and the ends of their dream. Once the state was established, the dream was fulfilled.

Rabbi Kook admired their love for the land and their dedication to it. However, he warned them that if they continued to be divorced from our Torah, their children would see devotion to the land as an unwelcome burden.

With the foundation of the state in 1948 until 1977, the Mizrachi-Religious Zionists were coalition partners with the Left. They resembled their secular counterparts in many ways. They were practical politicians and were interested mostly in preserving their piece of the pie. There was no Rabbi Kook on the national stage at the time to influence the party to be more than just that.

After the Six-Day War in 1967, and especially after the Yom Kippur war in 1973, there was a demand from National Religious youth for more than just practical politics.

Rabbi Kook, the son, was a spiritual giant, as was his father, and he provided the energy and ideas that breathed passion into the renewed movement. Power sharing and budgets were no longer enough for the younger generation of Religious Zionists.

As the various Zionist movements on the Left and Right lost ideological steam, a core of Religious Zionists insisted that the old Zionism was worth fighting for.

They are the last ones standing. If there is a revival of spirit, they will provide it.

What Is To Be Done About The Arab Threat?

Dr. Benny Morris, an Israeli historian, writes, "within 30-40 years, there will no longer be a Jewish majority in Israel and the 'Palestinian' population will do all to make life impossible for the Jews. As a result, all the Jews who can emigrate to the US and other places in the West will do so."

I don't know the source of his demographic projections. There is a robust debate amongst demographers about the future of population growth in this area. For the first time, this generation sees Jewish birth rate higher than Arab. Not only are Haredi/religious families having large families, but all Jewish sectors are. Secular families in Israel have the highest birthrates in the West.

There is an annual positive net immigration (Aliyah) to Israel, even as some Israelis choose to leave. There is still a large pool of potential immigrants from North America, France, Britain, South America, Ukraine, and Russia.

I recall the desperate warnings of some demographers just before the surprise Aliyah of a million Jews when the former Soviet Union had suddenly collapsed. The masses of Ethiopian Jews are a similar story. There were those who claimed that Israel as a Jewish majority had no future. Overnight, Israel became, unexpectedly, a different country.

It was Ben Gurion who said, "In Israel, if you don't believe in miracles, you are not a realist."

At the same time, many thousands of "Palestinian" Arabs flee the corrupt Palestinian Authority for anywhere that they can go. Chile has the largest Christian Arab community outside the Arab world, fleeing their Muslim neighbors. The Christian Arab population of Israel and of the PA / Gaza is rapidly shrinking. Communities with roots in the early days of Christianity are disappearing in the entire Middle East.

Muslims too are leaving if they can. In Gaza, those with

enough money to bribe officials are able to join the thousands each month that escape Hamas's rule.

With all that said, I agree that there is a demographic concern. Living with a considerable minority that clings to an unbridgeable animus towards the Jewish state is a real problem.

In the event of an existential threat beyond her borders, the army needs to be ready to deal simultaneously with a seditious population within her borders. This is what Israel faced in 1948. We thought that was forever behind us.

We were given a rude awakening in May 2021 as Hamas launched thousands of missiles and simultaneously thousands of Israeli Arabs attacked Jews from within. That is how the 1948 war began. We thought it was done and over.

I share the warning of the Left who speak of the danger of demographics that threaten the Jewish nature of the state. I find it puzzling then when the same Left opposes the deportation of illegal migrants and supports the right of thousands of Arabs to immigrate to Israel for "family reunion" (invariably Arab women marry Israeli Arab men. Why do these lovers never unite outside of Israel, the hated Jewish state?).

I have ample opportunity to meet Arabs as I speak their language. Some of them I like as individuals. I don't believe that they want to kill me though most do believe the same contrived historical narrative that my people stole their land.

They live a fantasy sustained by religion, society and culture. No matter how good they have it in the Jewish state, they nurture their gripe and wait for justice.

This is reflected in the anti-Israel politicians that they vote into the Knesset. So what is to be done?

First, the Arabs of the "territories": An international effort could help the Arabs of Gaza, Judea and Samaria join their many relatives abroad. Long lines would quickly form to flee the corrupt rule.

The US and the world community should pressure Hamas and the PA not to interfere. Those who claim to care about the "Palestinians" can open their doors as they have to millions of Syrians and others without a cent in their pockets.

Repeated polls show that over half the population of the PA and Hamas-ruled Gaza want to leave.

Help it happen. If there is even a little goodwill, it can. Whether there will be this cooperation or not, the terror leadership must know that their lives will not be worth living as long as Israelis suffer. No longer will Israelis be hostage to their whims. The rules will change.

The same applies to Israel proper. The Israeli Arab population has demonstrated that it is a time bomb. We dare not kick the problem under the rug any longer. Material benefits, complete human and civil rights are not the answer. We have not changed many minds. On the contrary, the resentment is more apparent today than in the past when conditions were less favorable for them. Love is never purchased; neither is allegiance nor even appreciation. We must face this.

Many Israeli Arabs would like to emigrate and join relatives abroad. We should buy their property if they have, and offer monetary incentives. We should facilitate relocation in every way. There should be a ministry responsible for this existential goal. It will be money better spent than managing a hostile population.

We need to express in every way that this is a Jewish country. Those who have problems with that might be happier elsewhere.

Zero tolerance for violence or the threat of violence against Jews or symbols of the Jewish country as experienced during the latest pogroms in May, 2021. The pathetic response to Arab violence at that time can only encourage more.

Expulsion without compensation will await those who lift their hands against Jews (hate crime).

We may not be aware of, as they are, but this is their jihad by varied means. Prison will no longer be where one can collect degrees, amass wealth and start a family. It will be a place one will not want to even contemplate.

Israeli universities will no longer be branches for terror groupies. Imams will no longer be allowed to preach hate and death for Jews.

Strict security screening will be required for certain employment and higher education.

We need to roll back a dangerous trend.

Instead of military service, national civilian service will be required.

Illegal possession of a weapon will be punished with expulsion.

The scourge of illegal building on national lands, protection rackets, agriculture theft, arson of farm lands and forests will be crimes not worth contemplating.

No more fear of "making things worse" and looking away.

Educate our people that we are the good guys with no nuance or apologetics. Teach our children who they are, and why it is the greatest honor to live in and defend our beloved, God given land.

There is no choice but to be clear and face our existential problems.

Next Year In A Rebuilt Jerusalem

Theodor Herzl famously said, "If you will it, it is not just a dream." I think I had one of those dreams yesterday, on Yom Kippur in shul. It must have been a mixture of hunger, fatigue and prayer that sent me a drowsy vision.

In my mind, I saw a combined Israeli naval and air operation successfully destroy Iran's nuclear capabilities and all forces returned safely to base. It was clear that Iran would order its proxies on Israel's borders to let loose with hundreds of thousands of deadly missiles they have been stockpiling for years. To save Israel's population and infrastructure from this mortal threat, a preemptive assault was launched, successfully eliminating over ninety percent of their targets. The entire terrorist leadership, down to the lowest level of command, was eliminated in surgical air strikes and commando raids.

With the heavy military activity going on, massive attacks by PA Arabs and personnel on Israeli settlements and transportation erupted in Judea and Samaria. Quick on its heels came the Arabs of East Jerusalem. Not to be left out of the jihad, the Arabs of Israel joined in.

The scenario of violent Arab uprisings in Israel was not a figment of my Yom Kippur stupor or a faded historical episode, but memories of a few months ago during the May 2021 pogroms.

My dream continued. As the Bible describes on a number of occasions as a hero arises to lead the people against an enemy, "the spirit of the Lord filled him."

Israeli military superiority and prowess were not the exciting part of the dream; rather that the Israelites were finally able to shrug off the chains of self doubt and apologetics as a "new spirit of God entered them."

This time the rioting Arabs were met by confident unhesitating Jews, determined to protect Jewish life, property and honor at all costs.

In the village of Awarta in Samaria, from where the terrorists who killed the Fogel family in the neighboring Itamar village came, there was a bloody confrontation. Some Arabs there approached the security fence of Itamar and began throwing gasoline bombs. One of the residents responded by shooting two of the attackers. Normally, this would mean the immediate arrest of the Jew and years in jail. This time it's different. A new spirit entered Israel.

Instead of protecting the Arab attackers, the Israeli authorities joined the Jews and chased the terrorists back into their village. There, many used weapons and gasoline bombs against the soldiers. Loudspeakers ordered them to deliver their weapons and to gather in the town square. All unarmed civilians would not be hurt.

Not yet aware of the renewed spirit of the Israelis, they played by the old rules and used their families as human shields and shot from behind them. This time Israeli soldiers acted like normal armies and were not deterred by the old game rules. Their own lives came before those of the enemy.

There was a firefight. Casualties were taken on both sides. Many Arabs, including civilians, were killed. It did not take long for word of the "massacre" to reach every Arab between the river and the sea. They were on their way, out.

Israeli Arabs were certain that the old rules still applied, especially for those holding the cherished/hated Israeli citizenship. In Lod, where Arabs torched hundreds of Jewish vehicles and homes and killed Jews just a few months ago, they were ready for round two. Alas, they faced the new spirit. Who knew?

This time, as the Arab mob streamed out of their mosques screaming "slaughter the Jew!", they were met by gunfire from within besieged Jewish homes. They in turn let loose with their own armory of illegal weapons just as the security forces appeared. Unlike in May, they did not arrest Jews for daring to defend themselves, but rather joined their Jewish brothers and sisters in repulsing the Arab mob.

The Arabs retreated into the main mosque, dragging a Jewish policewoman with them as a hostage. They were given a choice: release the hostage and be tried in a court of law or be killed on the spot and their families banished to Gaza.

They came out unarmed with white flags. One of them had

a pistol hidden, and hiding behind some others, opened fire on the police. They responded with a fusillade that killed him and a few near him. Some of the enraged Arabs rushed the police and they were cut down.

Word of this "massacre" reached every Israeli Arab within minutes. They were on their way out too.

In Jerusalem, Arabs attacked isolated Jewish communities on the mount of Olives and in the Old City. Same thing happened. The new spirit. They hurriedly packed their bags.

The result of these events was a mass exodus of Arabs from Judea and Samaria towards the Jordan border and Israeli Arabs in every direction. It was a deja vu of 1948.

In the War of Independence, one incident more than any other caused the panicked exodus of the enemy population; Deir Yasin. In that hostile, armed Arab village that controlled the entrance to Jerusalem, Jewish troops entered and demanded the Arabs disarm. A fight ensued and some Arabs used as human shields were killed. The story of Dir Yassin was exaggerated in order to stiffen Arab resolve to fight. It had the opposite effect and thus the exodus began.

It happened again. All Israeli villages that had been previously surrendered to the enemy in Gaza and Samaria were to be rebuilt and expanded immediately.

We were rid of our enemies from without and from within as the "spirit of the Lord rested upon Israel."

The confused, apologetic devil within was purged.

And then I woke up. I heard them singing. "Next year in a rebuilt Jerusalem."

Comments By Other Observers

"We are tired of fighting, we are tired of winning. We want a country that is fun to live in." ... *Ehud Olmert*

"Those who stand for nothing will fall for everything." ... *Alexander Hamilton*

"There is no security for Israel until it is secure in its own identity." *

"Those who don't fight wickedness, end up fighting those who do." ... *Dennis Prager*

"Israel has lost its moral certitude." *

"The settlers are the Jewish scapegoats for the Israelis." *

"The Jews won the election, the Israelis lost." ... *Shimon Peres, architect of the Oslo Accords.*

"The Oslo agreement was just a Trojan horse." ... *Faisal Husseini, PLO leader*

"Haj Amin Husseini (partner and ally of Hitler) was the spiritual father of the Palestinian people." ... *Yassar Arafat*

"In the exile, Jews were held hostage to their hosts. In Israel they made themselves hostage to their guests." *

"Arab culture has no good or bad, just strong and weak." *

"What drives Arab terror is not despair, but rather hope." *

"For Muslims, multiculturalism is a one-way street." *

"Arabs don't hate Jews because of Israel. They hate Israel because of Jews." *

"Only Arab despair can bring any chance of peace." *

"Our ties to Jerusalem go from antiquity to eternity." *

"Israel wasn't created to make Jew-haters happy." *

The secularization of Jihad – the "Palestinian" problem. *

"When the world condemns Israel you know they did something right." *

"The willingness of the Zionist to leave their synagogues in Gaza demonstrates that they have no God and therefore no religious connection to the land." … *Said by Iran after the destruction of the synagogues in Gaza (in the mass expulsion of Jews in 2005).*

"Within five years, we plan to destroy Israel." … *Arafat, 1996*

"Netanyahu – a great pilot flying nowhere". … *Moshe Feiglin*

"Better to have an Israel that is hated, than an Auschwitz that is tolerated." … *Rabbi Meir Kahane*

"Israel subsidizes its own suicide – maternity payments to Arabs." *

"Those who appease the crocodile will simply be eaten last." … *Winston Churchill*

"When Israel's leaders shook hands with murderers, Jews lost all direction except out." … *Moshe Feiglin*

"The Arab culture, at its core, is evil." … *Golda Meir*

"There will be peace with the Arabs when their mothers love their children more than they hate ours." … *Golda Meir*

"Israelis are constantly asked the same obnoxious question: 'How can you throw the Arabs out? Where will they go?' The answer is, if they don't care whom they kill, why are we obligated to care where they go?" ... *Jackie Mason, 2003*

"In the Middle East, either you are eating the meal or you are part of the menu." *

"The Arabs' hatred is the cause of their misery." *

"We have been experimenting with our survival to please our enemies." *

"It is a sin to deceive one's neighbor, it is a crime to deceive oneself." ... *The Kutzker Rebbe*

"I want peace so that there will be Israeliness. Peace is not an end in itself. It is the means with which to bring Israel from one era into another, to the era that I consider to be normal statehood: "Israelization" of society instead of its "Judaization." ... *Ron Pundak, a major architect of the Oslo Accords*

"History is not important." ... *Shimon Peres, father of the Oslo Accords*

"Ah, those who call evil good, and good evil, who present darkness as light, and light as darkness." ... *Isaiah 5:20*

---

* Original source of the comment is unknown.

Appendix

- Those Who Paid The Price Of Peace
- Maps

Those Who Paid The
Price Of Peace – To Date

This is a list of the people and their ages who have been murdered by the perpetrators of terrorism since 1993 (Oslo). Most of the victims were Israeli citizens, killed while going about their daily life or while serving their country in the IDF and other public services. Some were foreign workers and others were tourists. This information is provided by Israel's Ministry of Foreign Affairs (https://mfa.gov.il).

2021
St.-Sgt. Barel Shmueli, 21
Weerawat Krunboorirak, 44
Sikharin Sangamram, 24
Hava Vaknin, 73
Gershon Franko, 55
Miriam Arie, 84
Orly Liron, 52
Khalil Awad, 52
Nadin Awad, 16
Staff Sergeant Omer Tabib, 21
Ido Abigail, 5
Leah Yom Tov, 63
Nella Gurevitz, 52
Soumya Santosh, 32
Yehuda Guetta, 19

2020
Esther Horgan, 52
Rabbi Shai Ohayon, 39
Staff Sergeant Amit Ben Yigal, 21

2019
Nina Ganisdanova, 74
Rina Shnerb, 17
Dvir Sorek, 19
Rivka Jamil, 89
Pinchas Menachem Prezuazman, 21
Moshe Feder, 68
Ziad Alhamada, 49
Moshe Agadi, 58

Rabbi Achiad Ettinger, 47
Gal Keidan, 19
Ori Ansbacher, 19

2018
Yuval Mor Yosef, 20
Yoseph Cohen, 19
Amiad Israel, 4 days old
Mahmoud Abu Asba, 48
Kim Levengrond Yehezkel, 29
Ziv Hajbi, 35
Ari Fuld, 45
Sgt. Netanel Kahalani, 20
Yotam Ovadia, 31
Adiel Coleman, 30s
Capt. Ziv Daos, 21
Rabbi Itamar Ben-Gal, 29
Rabbi Raziel Shevach, 35

2017
Hodaya Asulin, 20
Or Arish, 25
Yussef Utman
First Sgt. Solomon Gabariya, 20
Kamil Shnaan, 22
Ha'il Satawi, 30
Haya Salomon
Elad Salomon, 35
Staff Sgt.Hadas Malka, 23
Yosef Salomon
Hannah Bladon, 23

Sgt. Elchai Taharlev, 20
Cadet Erez Orbach, 20
Cadet Shira Tzur, 20
Cadet Shir Hajaj, 22
Lt. Yael Yekutiel, 20

2016
Levana Melihi, 60
Michael Mark, 40
Hallel Yaffa Ariel, 13
Yosef Kirme, 29
Taylor Force, 28
Captain Eilav Gelman, 30
Tuvia Yanai Weissman, 18
Hadar Cohen, 19
Shlomit Krigman, 38
Dafna Meir, 38
Alon Bakal, 26
Shimon Ruimi, 30
Ilana Navaa, 39
Mila Mishayev, 33
Ido Ben Ari, 42
Michael Feige, 58

2015
Rabbi Rueven Birmajer, 45
Genadi Kaufman, 40
Ezra Schwartz, 18
Ya'acov Don, 51
Benjamin Yaakovovich, 19
Omri Levy, 19
Richard Lakin, 76
Aharon Banita-Bennet, 22
Rabbi Nehemia Lavi
Hadar Buchris, 21
Ziv Mizrahi, 20
Reuven Aviram, 51
Rabbi Aharon Yesiab, 32
Rabbi Yaakov Litman, 40
Netanel Litman, 18
Avraham Asher Hasano, 50
Omri Levy, 19
Rabbi Yeshayahu Krishevsky, 60
Haim Haviv, 78
Alon Govberg, 59

Richard Lakin, 76
Nahmia Lavi, 23
Aaron Bennet, 24
Eitam Henkin, early 30s
Naama Henkin, early 30s
Alexander Levlovitz, 64
Malachi Rosenfeld, 25
Danny Gonen, 25
Shalom Sherki, 25

2014
Rabbi Avraham S. Goldberg, 68
Rabbi Moshe Twersky, 60
Aryeh Kupinsky, 43
Rabbi Kalman Zeev Levine, 55
Master Sergant Zidan Sif, 30
Chaim Yechiel Rothman, 55
Dalia Lamkus, 25
Almog Shiloni, 20
Jedan Assad, 38
Chaya Zissel Braun, 3 months
Karen Mosquera, 22
Sergeant Netanel Maman, 21
Ze'ev Etzion, 50
Shahar Melamed, 43
Daniel Tregerman, 4
Lt. Hadar Goldin, 23
Maj. Benaya Sarel, 26
Staff Sgt. Liel Gidoni, 20
Cpt Liran Adir, 31
Staff Sgt. Noam Rosenthal, 20
Sgt. 1st Class Daniel Marash, 22
Capt. Omri Tal, 22
Staff Sgt. Shay Kushnir, 20
Staff Sgt. Eliav E. Haim Kahlon, 22
Meidan Maymon Biton, 20
Niran Cohen, 20
Staff Sgt. Adi Briga, 23
Maj. Tsafrir Baror, 32
Capt. Tsvi Kaplan, 28
Sgt. Gilad Rozenthal Yacoby, 21
Sgt. Oz Mandelovich, 21
Nissim Sean Carmeli, 21
Maj. Atmoz Greenberg
Sgt. Gilad Yaakovi, 21

Max Greenberg
Naftali Frankel, 16
Gilad Shaar, 16
Eyal Yifracah, 19
Shelley Dadon, 19
Baruch Mizrahi, 47

2013
Salah Shukri Abu Latyef, 21
Shlomi Cohen, 31
Eden Atias, 18
Seraya Ofer, 61
Gavriel Kobi, 20
Tomer Hazan, 20
Evyatar Borovsky, 31

2012
Lt. Boris Yarmulnik, 28
Cpl. Yosef Fartuk, 18
Alayaan Salem al-Nabari
Mirah Scharf, 25
Aharon Smadga, 40
Yitzhak Amselam, 22
Cpl Netanel Yahalomi, 20
Said Pashpasha, 36
Staff-Sgt Netanel Moshiashvili, 21

2011
Moshe Ami, 56
Asher Palmer, 25
Yonatan Palmer
Eliyahu Naim, 79
Yossi Shoshan, 38
Flora Gaz, 52
Moshe Gaz, 53
Shula Karlinsky, 54
Dov Karlinsky, 58
Yosef Levi, 58
Yitzhak Sela, 56
St-Sgt Moshe Naftali, 22
Chf Wrnt Offcr Pascal Avrahami, 49
Ben-Yosef Livnat, 24
Daniel Viflic, 16
Mary Jean Gardner, 55
Udi Fogel, 36

Ruth Fogel, 35
Yoav Fogel, 11
Elad Fogel, 4
Hadas Fogel, 3 months

2010
Kristine Luken, 46
Yitzhak Ames, 47
Talya Ames, 45
Avishai Shindler, 24
Kochava Chaim, 37
Sgt. Maj. Shuki Sofer, 39
Maj. Eliraz Peretz, 32
St.Sgt. Ilai Sviatkovsky, 21
Manee Singmueangphon, 34
First Sgt Ihab Khatib, 28

2009
Rabbi Meir Chai, 45
Gregory Rabinowitz, 56
Shlomo Nativ, 13
SWO Yehezkel Ramzarkar, 50
WO David Rabinowitz, 42

2008
WO Lutfi Nasraladin, 38
Irit Sheetrit, 39
Hani al-Mahdi, 27
Beber Vaknin, 58
Avraham Ozeri, 86
L-Cpl David Chriqui, 19
Lili Goren-Friedman, 54
Batsheva Unterman, 33
Jean Relevy, 68
Amnon Rosenberg, 51
Shuli Katz, 70
Jimmy Kadoshim, 48
Shimon Mizrahi, 53
Eli Wasserman, 51
Sgt. Menhash al-Banyat, 20
Sgt. Matan Ovdati, 19
Sgt. David Papian, 21
Oleg Lipson, 37
Lev Cherniak, 53
St.-Sgt. Sayef Bisan, 21

Segev Peniel Avihail, 15
Neria Cohen, 15
Yonatan Yitzhak Eldar, 16
Yehonadav Hirschfeld, 19
Yohai Lifshitz, 18
Doron Meherete, 26
Avraham David Moses, 16
Ro'i Roht, 18
St. Sgt Liran Banai, 20
St. Sgt. Doron Asulin, 20
St. Sgt. Eran Dan-Gur, 20
Roni Yihye, 47
Lyubov Razdolskaya, 73
L-Cpl Rami Zuari, 20
Carlos Andrés Chávez, 21

2007
Cpl. Ahikam Amihai, 20
Sgt. David Rubin, 21
Ido Zoldan, 29
Maj. Ehud Efrati, 34
Sgt. Ben Kubani, 20
St Sgt. Ben-Zion Haneman, 21
St Sgt. Arbel Reich , 21
Oshri Oz, 36
Shirel Friedman, 32
Erez Levanon, 42
Emi Haim Elmaliah, 32
Michael Ben Sa'adon, 27
Israel Zamalloa, 26

2006
Kinneret Ben Shalom Hajbi, 58
Eldar Abir, 48
Rafi Halevy, 63,
Helena Halevy 58
Re'ut Feldman, 20
Shaked Lasker, 16
Philip Balhasan, 45
Rozalia Beseneyi, 48
Pirosca Boda 50
Marcel Cohen, 73
Ariel Darhi, 31
Victor Erez, 60
Binyamin Haputa, 47

David Shaulov, 29
Lily Yunes, 42
Lior Anidzar, 26
Daniel Wultz, 16
Marwan Abed Shweika, 35
Lt. Hanan Barak, 20
Staff-Sgt. Pavel Slutzker, 20
Eliyahu Pinhas Asheri, 18
St.-Sgt. Osher Damari, 20
Dr. Daniel Yaakobi, 59
Angelo Frammartino, 24
St.-Sgt. Ro'i Farjoun, 21
Staff Sergeant Kiril Golenshein, 21
Fatima Slutsker, 57
Yaakov Yaakobov, 43

2005
Nissim Arbiv, 25
St.-Sgt. Yosef, Yossi Atia, 21
Gideon Rivlin, 50
Dror Gizri, 30
Ibrahim Kahili, 46
Munam Abu Sabia, 33
Ivan Shmilov, 53
Herzl Shlomo, 51
Ofer Tiri, 23
Ayala-Haya, (Ella) Abukasis, 17
Oded Sharon, 36,
Yitzhak Buzaglo, 40
Aryeh Nagar, 37
Yael Orbach, 28,
Ronen Ruevenov, 30
Odelia Hubara, 26
St.-Sgt. Dan Talasnikov, 21
Bi Shude, 46
Salah Ayash Imran, 57
Muhammed Mahmoud Jaroun
Sgt.-Maj. Avi Karouchi, 25
Yevgeny Reider, 28
Avihai Levy, 17
Rachel Ben Abu, 16
Nofar Horowitz, 16
Julia Voloshin, 31
Anya Lifshitz, 50
Cpl. Moshe Maor Jan, 21

Dana Gelkovitch, 22
Dov, 58, and Rachel Kol, 53
Shmuel Mett, 21
Sasson Nuriel, 55
Matat Rosenfeld Adler, 21
Kineret Mandel, 23
Oz Ben-Meir, 15
Michael Kaufman, 68
Pirhiya Machlouf, 53
Sabiha Nissim, 66
Jamil Qa'adan, 48
Ya'acov Rahmani, 68
Genia Poleis, 66
St.-Sgt. Yonatan Evron, 20
Hussam Fathi Mahajna, 36
Haim Amram, 26
Alexandra Garmitzky, 65
Daniel Golani, 45
Elia Rosen, 38
Keinan Tsuami, 20
Sgt. Nir Kahane, 20
Yosef, Yossi Shok, 35
Lt. Ori Binamo, 21

2004
Ro'i Arbel, 29
Cpl. Andrei Kegeles, 19
St.-Sgt. Tzur Or, 20
Gal Shapira, 29
BP St.-Sgt. Vladimir Trostinsky, 22
Avraham, Albert Balhasan, 28
Rose Boneh, 39
Hava Hannah, Anya Bonder, 38
Anat Darom, 23
Viorel Octavian Florescu, 42
Natalia Gamril, 53
Yechezkel Isser Goldberg, 41
Baruch, Roman Hondiashvili, 38
Dana Itach, 24
Mehbere Kifile, 35
Eli Zfira, 48
Ilan Avisidris, 41
Lior Azulai, 18
Yaffa Ben-Shimol, 57
Rahamim Doga, 38

Yehuda Haim, 48
St.-Sgt. Netanel Havshush, 20
Yuval Ozana, 32
Benayahu Zuckerman, 18
Sgt.-Maj. (res) Amir Zimmerman, 25
Eitan Kukoi, 30
Rima Novikov Kukoi, 25
Gil Abutbul, 38
Danny Assulin, 51
Avraham Avraham, 34
Zion Dahan, 30
Ophir Damari, 31
Moshe Hendler, 29
Mazal Marciano, 30
Avi Suissa, 56
Maurice Tubul, 30
Pinhas Avraham Zilberman, 45
George Khoury, 20
Yaakov Kobi Zagha, 40
BP Cpl. Kfir Ohayon, 20
BP Cpl. Yaniv Mashiah, 20
Tali Hatuel, 34
Hila Hatuel, 11
Hadar Hatuel, 9
Roni Hatuel, 7
Merav Hatuel, 2
Sgt. Adaron Amar, 20
Sgt. Aviad Deri, 21
Stf-Sgt. Ofer Jerbi, 21
Stf-Sgt. Ya'akov, Zelco Marviza, 25
Sgt. Kobi Mizrahi, 20
Staff-Sgt. Eitan Newman, 21
Cpl. Elad Cohen, 20
Sgt.-Maj. Aiman Ghadir, 24
Lt. Aviv Hakani, 23
Sgt. Za'ur, Zohar Smelev, 19
Sgt. Lior Vishinski, 20
St.-Sgt. Rotem Adam, 21
Sgt. Alexei Hayat, 21
Maj. Shachar Ben-Yishai, 25
Weerachai Wongput, 37
St.-Sgt. Roi Nissim, 20
Mordechai Yosepov, 49
Afik Zahavi, 4
Moshe Yohai, 63

Victor Kreiderman, 49
Sgt. Ma'ayan Na'im, 19
Shlomo Miller, 50
Shoshana Amos, 64
Aviel Atash, 3
Vitaly Brodsky, 52
Tamara Dibrashvilli, 70
Raisa Forer, 55
Larisa Gomanenko, 48
Denise Hadad, 50
Tatiana Kortchenko, 49
Rosita Lehman, 45
Karine Malka, 23
Nargiz Ostrovsky, 54
Maria Sokolov, 57
Roman Sokolovsky, 53
Tekele Tiroyaient, 33
Eliyahu Uzan, 58
Emmanuel Yosef, Yosefov, 28
Lance Cpl. Menashe Komemi, 19
Lance Cpl. Mamoya Tahio, 20
Capt. Tal Bardugo, 22
St.-Sgt. Nir Sami, 21
St.-Sgt. Israel Lutati, 20
Tiferet Tratner, 24
Dorit Aniso, 2
Yuval Abebeh, 4
St.-Sgt. Gilad Fisher, 22
Shlomit Batito, 36
Sgt. Victor Ariel, 20
Pratheep Nanongkham, 24
Assaf Greenwald, 27
Hafez al-Hafi, 39
Rotem Moriah, 27
Tzila Niv, 43
Gilad Niv, 11
Lior Niv, 3
Oleg Paizakov, 32
Ludmilla Paizakov, 30
Khalil Zeitounya, 10
Michal Alexander, 27
Roy Avisaf, 28
Einat Naor, 27
St.-Sgt. Yair Nisim Turgemann, 22
Sgt.-Maj. Moshe Almaliach, 35

Sgt. Michael Chizhik, 21
Tatiana Ackerman, 32
Leah Levine, 64
Shmuel Levy, 65
St.-Sgt. Nadav Kudinski, 20
Sgt. Araf Azbarga, 19
Sgt. Sa'id Jahaja, 19
Sgt. Hussein Abu Leil, 23
Adham Shehada, 19
Sgt. Tarek al-Ziadne, 20
Jitladda Tap-arsa, 19
Ariella Fahima, 39
Salem Sami al-Kimlat, 28

2003
Massoud Makhluf Alon, 72
Moshe Maurice Aharfi, 60
Mordechai Evioni, 52
Andrei Friedman, 30
Meir Haim, 74
Hannah Haimov, 53
Avi Kotzer, 43
Ramin Nasibov, 25
Staff Sgt. Mazal Orkobi, 20
Ilanit Peled, 32
Viktor Shebayev, 62,
Boris Tepalshvili, 51
Sapira Shoshana Yulzari-Yaffe, 46
Lilya Zibstein, 33
Amiram Zmora, 55
Igor Zobokov, 32
Krassimir Mitkov Angelov, 32
Steven Arthur Cromwell, 43
Ivan Gaptoniak, 46
Ion, Nelu Nicolae, 34
Guo Aiping, 47
Li Peizhong, 41
Mihai Sabau, 38
Zhang Minmin, 50
Eli Biton, 48
Cpl. (res) Mikhail Kazakov, 34
Netanel Ozeri, 34
Cpl. Ronald Berer, 20
Cpl. Assaf Bitan, 19,
St.-Sgt. Ya'akov Naim, 20

2nd Lt. Amir Ben-Aryeh, 21
St.-Sgt. Idan Suzin, 20
Maj. Shahar Shmul, 24
Cpl. Noam Bahagon, 20
Sgt. Tal Alexei Belitzky, 21
St.-Sgt. Doron Cohen, 21
Sgt. Itay Mizrahi, 20
Sgt. Doron Lev, 19
Maryam Atar, 27
Smadar Firstater, 16
Kamar Abu Hamed, 12
Daniel Haroush 16
Mordechai Hershko, 41
Tom Hershko, 15
Meital Katav, 20
Elizabeta Katzman, 16
Tal Kerman, 17
St.-Sgt. Eliyahu Laham, 22
Abigail Litle, 14
Yuval Mendelevitch, 13
St.-Sgt. Be'eri Oved, 21
Mark Takash, 54
Assaf Tzur, Zolinger, 17
Anatoly Biryakov, 20
Moran Shushan, 20
Rabbi Eli Horowitz, 52
Dina Horowitz, 50
St.-Sgt. Tomer Ron, 20
St.-Sgt. Assaf Moshe Fuchs, 21
Sgt.-Maj. (res) Ami Cohen, 27
Zion Boshirian, 51
St.-Sgt. Yigal Lifshitz, 20
St.-Sgt. Ofer Sharabi, 21
Lt. Daniel Mandel, 24
Zachar Rahamin Hanukayev, 39
Ahmed Salah Kara, 20
Cpl. Lior Ziv, 19
Alexander Kostyuk, 23
Ran Baron, 23
Dominique Caroline Hass, 29
Yanai Weiss, 46
Gideon Lichterman, 27
Zion David, 53
Gadi Levy 37
Dina Levy 31

Olga Brenner, 52
Yitzhak Moyal, 64
Nelly Perov, 55
Marina Tsahivershvili, 44
Shimon Ustinsky, 68
Roni Yisraeli, 34
Ghalab Tawil, 42
Kiryl Shremko, 22
Hassan Ismail Tawatha, 41
Avi Zerihan, 36
David Shambik, 26
Moran Menachem, 17
Sgt. Maj. (res) Assaf Abergil, 23
Sgt. Maj. (res) Udi Eilat, 38
Sgt. Maj. Boaz Emete, 24
Sgt. Maj. (res) Chen Engel, 32
St.-Sgt. Matan Gadri, 21
Sgt. Tamar Ben-Eliahu, 20
Alan Beer, 47
Eugenia Berman, 50
Elsa Cohen, 70
Zvi Cohen, 39
Roi Eliraz, 22
Alexander Kazaris, 77
Yaffa Mualem, 65
Yaniv Obayed, 22
Bat-El Ohana, 21
Anna Orgal, 55
Zippora Pesahovitch, 54
Bianca Shahrur, 62
Malka Sultan, 67
Bertine Tita, 75
Miriam Levy, 74
Avner Maimon, 51
St.-Sgt. Mordechai Sayada, 22
Noam Leibowitz, 7
Avner Mordechai, 58
Zvi Goldstein, 47
Amos Amit Mantin, 31
Sgt. Maj. Erez Ashkenazi, 21
Krastyu Radkov, 46
Mazal Afari, 65
Amir Simhon, 24
Cpl. Oleg Shaichat, 20
Roi Oren, 20

Haviv Dadon, 16
Yehezkel, Hezi Yekutieli, 43
Erez Hershkovitz, 18
Amatzia Nisanevitch, 22
Avraham Bar-Or, 12
Binyamin Bergman, 15
Yaakov Binder, 50
Feiga Dushinski, 50
Miriam Eisenstein, 20
Lilach Kardi, 22
Menachem Leibel, 24
Elisheva Meshulami, 16
Tehilla Nathanson, 3
Chava Nechama Rechnitzer, 19
Mordechai Reinitz, 49
Issachar Reinitz, 9
Maria Antonia Reslas, 39
Liba Schwartz, 54
Hanoch Segal, 65
Goldie Taubenfeld, 43
Shmuel Taubenfeld, 3 months
Rabbi Eliezer Weisfish, 42
Shmuel Wilner, 50
Shmuel Zargari, 11 months
Fruma Rahel Weitz, 73
Mordechai Laufer, 27
Tova Lev, 37
Shalom Har-Melekh, 25
St.-Sgt. Gabriel Uziel, 20
2nd PO Ra'anan Komemi, 23
SWO Haim Alfasi, 39
CWO Yaakov Ben-Shabbat, 39
Cpl. Mazi Grego, 19
Capt. Yael Kfir, 21
Cpl. Felix Nikolaichuk, 20
Sgt. Yonatan Peleg, 19
Sgt. Efrat Schwartzman, 19
Cpl. Prosper Twito, 20
Dr. David Appelbaum, 51
Nava Appelbaum, 20
David Shimon Avizadris, 51
Shafik Kerem, 27
Alon Mizrahi, 22
Gila Moshe, 40
Yehiel, Emil Tubol, 52

St.-Sgt. Avihu Keinan, 22
Eyal Yeberbaum, 27
Shaked Avraham, 7 months
Admiral (res) Ze'ev Almog, 71
Ruth Almog, 70
Moshe Almog, 43
Tomer Almog, 9
Assaf Staier, 11
Zvi Bahat, 35
Mark Biano, 29
Naomi Biano, 25
Hana Francis, 39
Mutanus Karkabi, 31
Sharbal Matar, 23
Osama Najar, 28
Nir Regev, 25
Irena Sofrin, 38
Bruria Zer-Aviv, 59
Bezalel Zer-Aviv, 30
Keren Zer-Aviv, 29
Liran Zer-Aviv, 4
Noya Zer-Aviv, 1
Lydia Zilberstein, 58
George Matar, 57
John Eric Branchizio, 37
John Martin Linde, Jr., 30
Mark T. Parson, 31
St.-Sgt. Erez Idan, 19
Sgt. Elad Pollack, 19
Sgt. Roi Ya'acov Solomon, 21
St.-Sgt. Alon Avrahami, 21
Sgt. Adi Osman, 19
Sgt. Sarit Schneor-Senior, 19
Sgt.-Maj. Shlomi Belsky, 23
St.-Sgt. Shaul Lahav, 20
Patricia Ter'n Navarrete, 33
Ilya Reiger, 58
Samer Fathi Afan, 25
Capt. Hagai Bibi, 24
Lt. Leonardo, Alex Weissman, 23
Adva Fisher, 20
St.-Sgt. Noam Leibowitz, 22
Cpl. Angelina Shcherov, 19
Cpl. Rotem Weinberger, 19

2002

Maj. Ashraf Hawash, 28
Sgt.-Maj. Ibrahim Hamadieh, 23
Sgt.-Mj. Hana, Eli Abu-Ghanem, 25
St.-Sgt. Mofid Sawaid, 25
Sgt. Elad Abu-Gani, 19
Avraham, Avi Boaz, 71
Yoela Chen, 45
Shahada Dadis, 30
Edward Bakshayev, 48
Anatoly Bakshayev, 63
Aharon Ben Yisrael-Ellis, 32
Dina Binayev, 48
Boris Melikhov, 56
Avi Yazdi, 25
Sarah Hamburger, 79
Svetlana Sandler, 56
Pinhas Tokatli, 81
Miri Ohana, 45
Yael Ohana, 11
SSMaj. Moshe Majos Meconen, 33
Moran Amit, 25
Atala Lipobsky, 78
Lt. Keren Rothstein, 20
Cpl. Aya Malachi, 18
St.-Sgt. Ron Lavie, 20
St.-Sgt. Moshe Peled, 20
St.-Sgt. Asher Zaguri, 21
St.-Sgt. Lee Nahman Akunis, 20
Nehemia Amar, 15
Keren Shatsky, 15
Rachel Theler, 16
Policeman Ahmed Mazarib, 32
Ahuva Amergi, 30
Maj. Mor Elraz, 25
St.-Sgt. Amir Mansouri, 21
Lt. Moshe Eini, 21
St.-Sgt. Benny Kikis, 20
St.-Sgt. Mark Podolsky, 20
St.-Sgt. Erez Turgeman, 20
St.-Sgt. Tamir Atsmi, 21
St.-Sgt. Michael Oxsman, 21
Valery Ahmir, 59
Avraham Fish, 65
Aharon Gorov, 46

PO 1st Sgt. Galit Arbiv, 21
Gad Rejwan, 34
St.-Sgt. Haim Bachar, 20
Sgt. Ya'acov Avni, 20
JPD Chief-Supt. Moshe Dayan, 46
Shlomo Nehmad, 40
Gafnit Nehmad, 32
Shiraz Nehmad, 7
Liran Nehmad, 3
Shaul Nehmad, 15
Lidor Ilan, 12
Oriah Ilan, 18 months
Tzofia Ya'arit Eliyahu, 23
Ya'akov Avraham Eliyahu, 7 months
Avi Hazan, 37
Ariel Hovav, 25
David Damelin, 29
1st Sgt. (res) Rafael Levy, 42
Sgt.-Maj. (res) Avraham Ezra, 38
Eran Gad, 24
Sgt.-Maj. (res) Yochai Porat, 26
Sgt.-Maj. (res) Kfir Weiss, 24
Sergei Butarov, 33
Vadim Balagula, 32
Didi Yitzhak, 66
Sgt. Steven Koenigsburg, 19
PO FSM Salim Barakat, 33
Yosef Habi, 52
Eli Dahan, 53
Devorah Friedman, 45
Maharatu Tagana, 85
1st Lt. Pinhas Cohen, 23
Cpl. (res) Alexander Nastarenko, 37
Arik Krogliak, 18
Eran Picard, 18
Ariel Zana, 18
St.-Sgt. Edward Korol, 20
Avia Malka, 9 months
Israel Yihye, 27
Limor Ben-Shoham, 27
Nir Borochov, 22
Danit Dagan, 25
Livnat Dvash, 28
Tali Eliyahu, 26
Uri Felix, 25

Dan Imani, 23
Natanel Kochavi, 31
Baruch Lerner, 29
Orit Ozerov, 28
Avraham Haim Rahamim, 28
St.-Sgt. Kobi Eichelboim, 21
Eyal Lieberman, 42
Yehudit Cohen, 33
Ofer Kanarick, 44
Alexei Kotman, 29
Lynne Livne, 49
Atara Livne, 15
Lt. German Rozhkov, 25
Lt. Gil Badihi, 21
St.-Sgt. Matan Biderman, 21
St.-Sgt. Ala Hubeishi, 21
Sgt. Rotem Shani, 19
Noa Auerbach, 18
1st Lt. Tal Zemach, 20
Sgt. Michael Altfiro, 19
St.-Sgt. Shimon Edri, 20
SWO Meir Fahima, 40
Cpl. Aharon Revivo, 19
Alon Goldenberg, 28
Mogus Mahento, 75
Bella Schneider, 53
Gadi Shemesh, 34
Tzipi Shemesh, 29
Yitzhak Cohen, 48
Esther Klieman, 23
Avi Sabag, 24
Major Cengiz Soytunc
Catherine Berruex
Shula Abramovitch, 63
David Anichovitch, 70
Sgt.-Maj. Avraham Beckerman, 25
Shimon Ben-Aroya, 42
Andre Fried, 47
Idit Fried, 47
Miriam Gutenzgan, 82
Ami Hamami, 44
Perla Hermele, 79
Dvora Karim, 73
Michael Karim, 78
Yehudit Korman, 70

Marianne Lehmann Zaoui, 77
Lola Levkovitch, 85
Furuk Na'imi, 62
Eliahu Nakash, 85
Irit Rashel, 45
Yulia Talmi, 87
St.-Sgt. Sivan Vider, 20
Ernest Weiss, 79
Eva Weiss, 75
Meir, George Yakobovitch, 76
Chanah Rogan, 92
Zee'v Vider, 50
Alter Britvich, 88
Frieda Britvich, 86
Sarah Levy-Hoffman, 89
Anna Yakobovitch, 78
Rachel and David Gavish, 50
Avraham Gavish, 20
Yitzhak Kanner, 83
Tuvia Wisner, 79
Michael Orlinsky, 70
Lt. Boaz Pomerantz, 22
St.-Sgt. Roman Shliapstein, 22
Rachel Levy, 17
Haim Smadar, 55
BP Sgt.-Maj. Constantine Danilov, 23
Suheil Adawi, 32
Dov Chernevroda, 67
Shimon Koren, 55
Ran Koren, 18
Gal Koren, 15
Moshe Levin, 52
Danielle Manchell, 22
Orly Ofir, 16
Aviel Ron, 54
Ofer Ron, 18
Anat Ron, 21
Ya'akov Shani, 53
Adi Shiran, 17
Daniel Carlos Wegman, 50
Carlos Yerushalmi, 52
Sgt.-Maj. Ofir Roth, 22
Tomer Mordechai, 19
Maj. Moshe Gerstner, 29
Rachel Charhi, 36

Border Police Supt. Patrick Pereg, 30
Sgt.-Maj. (res) Einan Sharabi, 32
Lt. Nissim Ben-David, 22
St.-Sgt. Gad Ezra, 23
Sgt. Merom Fisher, 19
Sgt. Ro'i Tal, 21
Sgt. Oded Kornfein, 20
St.-Sgt. Nisan Avraham, 26
St.-Sgt. Matanya Robinson, 21
Sgt. Shmuel Weiss, 19
Maj. (res) Oded Golomb, 22
Capt. (res) Ya'akov Azoulai, 30
Lt. (res) Dror Bar, 28
Lt. (res) Eyal Yoel, 28
1st Sgt. (res) Tiran Arazi, 33
1st Sgt. (res) Yoram Levy, 33
1st Sgt. (res) Avner Yaskov, 34
Sgt. 1st Cl (res) Ronen Alshochat, 27
1st Cl (res) Eyal Eliyahu Azouri, 27
Sgt. 1st Cl (res) Amit Busidan, 22
Sgt. 1st Cl (res) Menashe Hava, 23
Sgt. 1st Cl (res) Shmuel Meizlish, 27
Sgt. 1st Cl (res) Eyal Zimmerman, 22
Maj. Assaf Assoulin, 30
St.-Sgt. Gedalyahu Malik, 21
Avinoam Alfia, 26
Sgt.-Maj. (res) Shlomi Ben Haim, 27
Sgt.-Maj. (res) Nir Danieli, 24
BP Lance Cpl. Keren Franco, 18
Sgt.-Maj. (res) Ze'ev Hanik, 24
BP Lance Cpl. Noa Shlomo, 18
PWO Shimshon Stelkol, 33
Sgt. Michael Weissman, 21
Lt. Dotan Nahtomi, 22
BP St.-Sgt. David Smirnoff, 22
Nissan Cohen, 57
Rivka Fink, 75
Suheila Hushi, 48
Yelena Konrab, 43
Ling Chang Mai, 34
Chai Siang Yang, 32
BP St.-Sgt. Uriel Bar-Maimon, 21
Sgt. Maj. Nir Krichman, 22
Danielle Shefi, 5
Arik Becker, 22

Katrina, Katya Greenberg, 45
Ya'acov Katz, 51
Major Avihu Ya'akov, 24
Esther Bablar, 54
Yitzhak Bablar, 57
Avi Bayaz, 26
Regina Malka Boslan, 62
Edna Cohen, 61
Rafael Haim, 64
Pnina Hikri, 60
Nawa Hinawi, 51
Rahamim Kimhi, 58
Nir Lovatin, 31
Shoshana Magmari, 51
Dalia Masa, 56
Rassan Sharouk, 60
Israel Shikar, 49
Anat Teremforush, 36
Nisan Dolinger, 43
Yosef Haviv, 70
Victor Tatrinov, 63
Arkady Vieselman, 40
Elmar Dezhabrielov, 16
Gary Tauzniaski, 65
Sgt. 1st Cl (res) Oren Tzelnik, 23
Ruth Peled, 56
Sinai Keinan, 14 months
Albert Maloul, 50
Netanel Riachi, 17
Gilad Stiglitz, 14
Avraham Siton, 17
Cpl. Liron Avitan, 19
Cpl. Avraham Barzilai, 19
Cpl. Dennis Bleuman, 20
St.-Sgt. Eliran Buskila, 21
St.-Sgt. Zvi Gelberd, 20
Sgt. Violetta Hizgayev, 20
St.-Sgt. Ganadi Issakov, 21
Sgt. Sariel Katz, 21
Cpl. Vladimir Morari, 19
Sgt. Yigal Nedipur, 21
Sgt. Dotan Reisel, 22
St.-Sgt. David Stanislavksy, 23
Sgt. Sivan Wiener, 19
Zion Agmon, 50

Adi Dahan, 17
Shimon Timsit, 35
Erez Rund, 18
St.-Sgt. Eyal Sorek, 23
Yael Sorek, 24
SSMaj. (res) Shalom Mordechai, 35
Hadar Hershkowitz, 14
SSt. Haim Yehezkel Gutman, 22
St.-Sgt. Alexei Gladkov, 20
Lt. Anatoly Krasik, 22
Boaz Aluf, 54
Shani Avi-Zedek, 15
Leah Baruch, 59
Mendel Bereson, 72
Rafael Berger, 28
Michal Biazi, 24
Tatiana Braslavsky, 41
Galila Bugala, 11
Raisa Dikstein, 67
Dr. Moshe Gottlieb, 70
Baruch Gruani, 60
Orit Hayla, 21
Helena Ivan, 63
Iman Kabha, 26
Shiri Negari, 21
Gila Nakav, 55
Yelena Plagov, 42
Liat Yagen, 24
Rahamim Zidkiyahu
Noa Alon, 60
Gal Eisenman, 5
Michal Franklin, 22
Tatiana Igelski, 43
Hadassah Jungreis, 20
Gila Sara Kessler, 19
Shmuel Yerushalmi, 17
Maj. Shlomi Cohen, 26
St.-Sgt. Yosef Talbi, 20
Rachel Shabo, 40
Neria Shabo, 16
Zvika Shabo, 12
Avishai Shabo, 5
Yosef Twito, 31
Capt. Hagai Lev, 24
Galila Ades, 42

Yonatan Gamliel, 16
Keren Kashani, 29
Sarah Tiferet Shilon, 8 months
Gal Shilon, 32
Zilpa Kashi, 65
Ilana Siton, 35
Yocheved Ben-Hanan, 21
Lt. Elad Grenadier, 21
Adrian Andres, 30
Boris Shamis, 25
Xu Hengyong, 39
Li Bin, 33
Dmitri Pundikov, 33
Rabbi Elimelech Shapira, 43
St.-Sgt. Elazar Lebovitch, 21
Rabbi Yosef Dikstein, 45
Hannah Dikstein, 42
Shuv'el Zion Dikstein, 9
Shlomo Odesser, 60
Mordechai Odesser, 52
David Diego Ladowski, 29
Levina Shapira, 53
Marla Bennett, 24
Benjamin Blutstein, 25
Dina Carter, 37
Janis Ruth Coulter, 36
David Gritz, 24
Daphna Spruch, 61
Revital Barashi, 30
Shani Ladani, 27
Mordechai Yehuda Friedman, 24
Sari Goldstein, 21
Maysoun Amin Hassan, 19
Marlene Menahem, 22
Sgt.-Maj. Roni Ghanem, 28
Sgt. Yifat Gavrieli, 19
Sgt. Omri Goldin, 20
Adelina Kononen, 37
Rebecca Roga, 40
Yekutiel Amitai, 34
Nizal Awassat, 52
Avi Wolanski, 29
Avital Wolanski, 27
Yafit Herenstein, 31
St.-Sgt. Kevin Cohen, 19

1st Lt. Malik Grifat, 24
Sgt. Aviad Dotan, 21
David Buhbut, 67
Yosef Ajami, 36
Police Sgt. Moshe Hezkiyah, 21
Solomon Hoenig, 79
Yossi Mamistavlov, 39
Yaffa Shemtov, 49
Rosanna Siso, 63
Ofer Zinger, 29
Jonathan Yoni Jesner, 19
Shlomo Yitzhak Shapira, 48
Capt. Harel Marmelstein, 23
St.-Sgt. Ari Weiss, 21
Oded Wolk, 51
Sa'ada Aharon, 71
Osnat Abramov, 16
St.-Sgt. Liat Ben-Ami, 20
Ofra Burger, 56
Cpl. Ilona Hanukayev, 20
Ashati Indelau, 50
Suad Jaber, 23
Iris Lavi, 68
SMaj. (res) Eliezer Moskovitch, 40
St.-Sgt. Nir Nahum, 20
Sgt. Esther Pisahov, 19
St.-Sgt. Aiman Sharuf, 20
Anat Shimshon, 34
Cpl. Sharon Tubol, 19
Maj. (res) Tamir Masad, 41
Lt. Matan Zagron, 22
Sgt.-Maj. Amihud Hasid, 32
Orna Eshel, 53
Linoy Saroussi, 14
Hadas Turgeman, 14
Julio Pedro Magram, 51
Gastón Perpiñal, 15
Assaf Tzfira, 18
Amos Sa'ada, 52
Sgt.-Maj. Madin Grifat, 23
Revital Ohayon, 34
Matan Ohayon, 5
Noam Ohayon, 4
Yitzhak Dori, 44
Tirza Damari, 42

Col. Dror Weinberg, 38
BPO Ch.-Supt. Samih Sweidan, 31
Sgt. Tomer Nov, 19
Sgt. Gad Rahamim, 19
St.-Sgt. Netanel Machluf, 19
St.-Sgt. Yeshayahu Davidov, 20
Sgt. Igor Drobitsky, 20
Cpl. David Marcus, 20
Lt. Dan Cohen, 22
Yitzhak Buanish, 46
Alexander Zwitman, 26
Alexander Dohan, 33
Esther Galia, 48
Hodaya Asraf, 13
Marina Bazarski, 46
Hadassah Yelena Ben-David, 32
Sima Novak, 56
Kira Perlman, 67
Ilan Perlman, 8
Yafit Ravivo, 14
Ella Sharshevsky, 44
Michael Sharshevsky, 16
Mircea Varga, 25
Dikla Zino, 22
Sgt.-Maj. Shigdaf Shai Garmai, 30
Noy Anter, 12
Dvir Anter, 14
Albert, Avraham de Havila, 60
Haim Amar, 56
Ehud Yehuda Avitan, 54
Mordechai Avraham, 44
Ya'acov Lary, 35
David Peretz, 48
Shaul Zilberstein, 36
Corp. Keren Ya'akobi, 19
Sgt. Maor Kalfon, 19
Rabbi Yitzhak Arama, 40
St.-Sgt. Noam Apter, 23
Pvt. Yehuda Bamberger, 20
Gavriel Hoter, 17
Zvi Zieman, 18

2001
Ron Tzalah, 32
Ofir Rahum, 16

Motti Dayan, 27
Etgar Zeituny, 34
Akiva Pashkos, 45
Arye Hershkowitz, 55
Dr. Shmuel Gillis, 42
Lior Attiah, 23
St.-Sgt. Rujayah Salameh, 23
Tzachi Sasson, 35
Simcha Shitrit, 30
Staff-Sgt. Ofir Magidish, 20
Sgt. David Iluz, 21
Sgt. Julie Weiner, 21
Sgt. Rachel Levy, 19
Sgt. Kochava Polanski, 19
Cpl. Alexander Manevich, 18
Cpl. Yasmin Karisi, 18
Mordechai Shefer, 55
Claude Knap, 29
Naftali Dean, 85
Shlomit Ziv, 58
Yevgenya Malchin, 70
Baruch Cohen, 59
Shalhevet Pass, 10 months
Eliran Rosenberg-Zayat, 15
Naftali Lanzkorn, 13
Staff Sgt. Ya'akov Krenschel, 23
Dina Guetta, 42
Sgt. Danny Darai, 20
Stanislav Sandomirsky, 38
Dr. Mario Goldin, 53
Sgt. Shlomo Elmakias, 20
Simcha Ron, 60
Assaf Hershkowitz, 30
Arnaldo Agranionic, 48
Yossi Ish-Ran, 14
Kobi Mandell, 14
Constantin Straturula, 52
Virgil Martinesc, 29
Idit Mizrahi, 20
Tirza Polonsky, 66
Miriam Waxman, 51
David Yarkoni, 53
Yulia Tratiakova, 21
Vladislav Sorokin, 34
Lt. Yair Nebenzahl, 22

Asher Iluz, 33
Yosef Alfasi, 50
Gilad Zar, 41
Sarah Blaustein, 53
Esther Alvan, 20
Zvi Shelef, 63
Marina Berkovizki, 17
Roman Dezanshvili, 21
Ilya Gutman, 19
Anya Kazachkov, 16
Katherine Kastaniyada-Talkir, 15
Aleksei Lupalu, 16
Mariana Medvedenko, 16
Irina Nepomneschi, 16
Yelena Nelimov, 18
Yulia Nelimov, 16
Raisa Nimrovsky, 15
Pvt. Diez Dani Normanov, 21
Simona Rodin, 18
Ori Shahar, 32
Liana Sakiyan, 16
Maria Tagilchev, 14
Irena Usdachi, 18
Sergei Pancheskov, 20
Yael-Yulia Sklianik, 15
Jan Bloom, 25
Yevgenia Dorfman, 15
Yehuda Shoham, 5 months
Father Georgios Tsibouktzakis, 34
Lt.Col. Yehuda Edri, 45
Dan Yehuda, 35
Doron Zisserman, 38
Ilya Krivitz, 62
Sgt. Aviv Iszak, 19
Sgt. Ofir Kit, 19
Ekaterina Katya Weintraub, 27
Aharon Obadyan, 41
Yair Har Sinai, 51
Eliahu Na'aman, 32
Capt. Shai Shalom Cohen, 22
Yehezkel Hezi Mualem, 49
David Cohen, 28
Cpl. Hanit Arami, 19
St.Sgt. Avi Ben Harush, 20
Yuri Gushchin, 18

Ronen Landau, 17
Tehiya Bloomberg, 40
Yitzhak Snir, 51
Wael Ghanem, 32
Zohar Shurgi, 40
Giora Balash, 60
Zvika Golombek, 26
Shoshana Yehudit Greenbaum, 31
Tehila Maoz, 18
Frieda Mendelsohn, 62
Michal Raziel, 16
Malka Roth, 15
Mordechai Schijveschuurder, 43
Tzira Schijveschuurder, 41
Ra'aya Schijveschuurder, 14
Avraham Yitzhak Schijveschuurder, 4
Hemda Schijveschuurder, 2
Lily Shimashvili, 33
Tamara Shimashvili, 8
Yocheved Shoshan, 10
Aliza Malka, 17
Maj. Gil Oz, 30
St.-Sgt. Kobi Nir, 21
Tzahi Grabli, 19
Sharon Ben-Shalom, 26
Yaniv Ben-Shalom, 27
Doron Sviri, 20
Dov Rosman, 58
Meir Lixenberg, 38
Oleg Sotnikov, 35
Amos Tajouri, 60
Lt. Erez Merhavi, 23
Ya'akov Hatzav, 42
Sima Franko, 24
Dr. Yigal Goldstein, 47
Morel Derfler, 45
Sgt. Daniel Yifrah, 19
BP Sgt. Tzachi David, 19
St.-Sgt. Andrei Zledkin, 26
Ruth Shua'i, 46
Meir Weisshaus, 23
Sgt. David Gordukal, 23
Sarit Amrani, 26
Salit Sheetrit, 28
Cpl. Liron Harpaz, 19

Assaf Yitzhaki, 20
Sgt. Tali Ben-Armon, 19
Haim Ben-Ezra, 76
Sergei Freidin, 20
Hananya Ben-Avraham, 46
Yair Mordechai, 43
Tourism Min. Rechavam Ze'evy, 75
Lior Kaufman, 30
St.-Sgt. Yaniv Levy, 22
Ayala Levy, 39
Smadar Levy, 23
Lydia Marko, 63
Sima Menachem, 30
St.-Sgt. Raz Mintz, 19
Shoshana Ben-Yishai, 16
Menashe Meni Regev, 14
Capt. (res) Eyal Sela, 39
Hadas Abutbul, 39
Aharon Ussishkin, 50
St.-Sgt. Barak Madmon, 26
Noam Gozovsky, 23
Michal Mor, 25
Etty Fahima, 45
1st Sgt. Yaron Pikholtz, 20
Inbal Weiss, 22
Yehiav Elshad, 28
Samuel Milshevsky, 45
Assaf Avitan, 15
Michael Moshe Dahan, 21
Israel Ya'akov Danino, 17
Yosef El-Ezra, 18
Sgt. Nir Haftzadi, 19
Yuri Yoni Korganov, 20
Golan Turgeman, 15
Guy Vaknin, 19
Adam Weinstein, 14
Moshe Yedid-Levy, 19
Ido Cohen, 17
Prof. Baruch Singer, 51
Tatiana Borovik, 23
Mara Fishman, 51
Ina Frenkel, 60
Riki Hadad, 30
Ronen Kahalon, 30
Samion Kalik, 64

Mark Khotimliansky, 75
Cecilia Kozamin, 76
Yelena Lomakin, 62
Rosaria Reyes, 42
Yitzhak Ringel, 41
Rassim Safulin
Leah Strick, 73
Faina Zabiogailu, 64
Mikhail Zaraisky, 71
Yair Amar, 13
Esther Avraham, 42
BP CWO Yoel Bienenfeld, 35
Moshe Gutman, 40
Avraham Nahman Nitzani, 17
Yirmiyahu Salem, 48
Israel Sternberg, 46
David Tzarfati, 38
Hananya Tzarfati, 32
Ya'akov Tzarfati, 64
Sgt. Michael Sitbon, 23

2000
Sgt. David Biri, 19
BP Supt. Yossi Tabaja, 27
BP Cpl. Yosef Madhat, 19
Wichlav Zalsevsky, 24
Sgt. Max Hazan, 20
Bachor Jean, 54
Hillel Lieberman, 36
First Cpl. Yosef Avrahami
First Sgt. Vadim Novesche, 33
Rabbi Binyamin Herling, 64
Marik Gavrilov, 25
Eish-Kodesh Gilmor, 25
Amos Machlouf, 30
Lt. David-Hen Cohen, 21
Sgt. Shlomo Adshina, 20
Maj. (res) Amir Zohar, 34
Ayelet Shahar Levy, 28
Hanan Levy, 33
Noa Dahan, 25
Sgt. Shahar Vekret, 20
Sgt. 1st Class Avner Shalom, 28
Sarah Leisha, 42
Cpl. Elad Wallenstein, 18

Cpl. Amit Zanna, 19
Gabi Zaghouri, 36
St.-Sgt. Baruch Snir Flum, 21
St.-Sgt. Sharon Shitoubi, 21
Miriam Amitai, 35
Gavriel Biton, 34
Itamar Yefet, 18
Shoshana Reis, 21
Meir Bahrame, 35
Lt. Edward Matchnik, 21
Sgt. Samar Hussein, 19
Maj. Sharon Arameh, 25
Ariel Jeraffi, 40
Rina Didovsky, 39
Eliyahu Ben-Ami, 41
Sgt. Tal Gordon, 19
Eliahu Cohen, 29
Capt. Gad Marasha, 30
BP Sgt.-Maj. Yonatan Vermullen, 29
Binyamin Zeev Kahane
Talia Kahane

1999
Sergeant Yehoshua Gavriel, 25
Yehiel Finfeter, 25
Sharon Steinmetz, 21

1998
Yael Meivar, 25
David Ktorza, 40
Haim Kerman, 28
Harel Bin-Nun, 18
Shlomo Liebman, 24
Rabbi Shlomo Ra'anan, 63
IDF soldier Michal Adato, 19
Itamar Doron, 24
Danny Vargas, 29
Sergeant Alexey Neykov, 19

1997
Michal Avrahami, 32
Yael Gilad, 32
Anat Winter-Rosen, 32
Staff-Sgt. Sharon Edri
Hagit Zavitzky, 23

Liat Kastiel, 23
Lev Desyatnik, 60
Regina Giber, 76
Valentina Kovalenko, 67
Shmuel Malka, 44
David Nasco, 44
Muhi A-din Othman, 33
Simha Fremd, 92
Grisha Paskhovitz, 15
Leah Stern, 50
Rachel Tejgatrio, 80
Liliya Zelezniak, 47
Shalom, Golan Zevulun, 52
Mark Rabinowitz, 80
Eli Adourian, 49
Ilia Gazrach, 73
Baruch Ostrovsky, 84
Yael Botwin, 14
Sivan Zarka, 14
Smadar Elhanan, 14
Rami Kozashvili, 20
Eliahu Markowitz, 40
Gabriel Hirschberg, 26

1996
Sgt. Yaniv Shimel
Major Oz Tibon
Staff Sgt. Ehud Tal, 21
Daniel Biton, 42
Yitzhak Elbaz, 57
Boris Sharpolinsky, 64
Semion Trakashvili, 60
Yitzhak Yakhnis, 54
Peretz Gantz, 61
Anatoly Kushnirov, 36
Jana Kushnirov, 37
Masuda Amar, 59
Swietlana Gelezniak, 32
Celine Zaguri, 19
Navon Shabo, 22
Michael Yerigin, 16
Matthew Eisenfeld, 25
Sara Duker, 23
Wael Kawasmeh, 23
Ira Yitzhak Weinstein, 53

Sgt. Yonatan Barnea, 20
St-Sgt. Gavriel Krauss, 24
St.-Sgt. Gadi Shiloni, 22
Cpl. Moshe Reuven, 19
St.-Sgt. Maj. (res) Arye Barashi, 39
Cpl. Iliya Nimotin, 19
Cpl. Merav Nahum, 19
Sgt. Sharon Hanuka, 19
Arik Gaby, 16
Sgt. Hofit Ayyash, 20
Flora Yehiel, 28
Maya Birkan, 59
Naima Zargary, 66
Gavriel Shamashvili, 43
Shemtov Sheikh, 63
Anna Shingeloff, 36
Raya Daushvili, 55
George Yonan, 38
Sarina Angel, 45
Gidi Taspanish, 23
Valerian Krasyon, 44
Dominic Lunca, 29
Daniel Patenka, 33
Marian Grefan, 40
Mirze Gifa, 39
Dimitru Kokarascu, 43
Imar Ambrose, 51
Sgt. Yoni Levy, 21
Sgt. Haim Amedi, 19
Senior NCO Uzi Cohen, 54
Bat-Hen Shahak, 15
Hadas Dror, 15
Kobi Zaharon, 13
Inbar Atiya, 21
Dan Tversky, 58
Dana Gutman, 14
Yovav Levy, 13
Leah Mizrahi, 60
Tali Gordon, 24
Rahel Sela, 82
Sylvia Bernstein, 73
Gail Belkin, 48
St.-Sgt. Assaf Wachs, 21
David Baum, 17
Yaron Unger, 26

Efrat Unger, 25
First-Sgt. Meir Alush, 40
Staff Sgt. (res) Asher Berdugo, 22
Sgt. Ashraf Shibli, 20
Cpl. (res) Ya'acov Turgeman
Uri Munk, 53
Rachel Munk, 24
Ze'ev Munk
Etta Tzur, 48
Ephraim Tzur, 12

1995
Ofra Felix, 20
Lt. David Ben-Zino, 20
Lt. Adi Rosen, 20
Lt. Yuval Tuvya, 22
Sgt.-Maj. Anan Kadur, 24
Staff-Sgt. Damian Rosovski, 20
Staff-Sgt. Yehiel Sharvit, 21
Staff-Sgt. Yaron Blum, 20
Sgt. Maya Kopstein, 19
Sgt. Daniel Tzikuashvili, 19
Sgt. Avi Salto, 19
Sgt. Rafael Mizrahi, 19
Sgt. Eran Gueta, 20
Cpl. Soli Mizrahi, 18
Cpl. David Hasson, 18
Cpl. Amir Hirschenson, 18
Cpl. Gilad Gaon, 18
Cpl. Ilie Dagan, 18
Cpl. Eitan Peretz, 18
Shabtai Mahpud, 34
Lt. Eyal Levy, 20
Cpl. Yaniv Weiser, 18
Yevgeny Gromov, 32
Rafael Cohen, 35
Nahum Hoss, 32
Yehuda Fartush, 41
Police Insp. Nitzan Cohen, 22
Sgt.-Maj. Jamal Suwitat
Staff-Sgt. Yuval Regev, 20
Staff-Sgt. Meir Scheinwald, 20
Sgt. Itai Diener, 19
Sgt. Zvi Narbat, 19
Sgt. Netta Sufrin, 20

Cpl. Tal Nir, 19
Sgt. Avraham Arditi, 19
Alisa Flatow, 20
Ohad Bachrach, 18
Ori Shahor, 20
Moshe Shkedi, 75
Rahel Tamari, 65
Zviya Cohen, 62
Zahava Oren, 60
Nehama Lubowitz, 61
Mordechai Tovia, 37
Rivka Cohen, 26
Hannah Naeh, 56
Joan Davenney, 46
PC Super. Noam Eisenman, 35
Daniel Frei, 28

1994
Moshe Becker
Grigory Ivanov
Ilan Sudri
Naftali Sahar
Noam Cohen, 28
Yuval Golan
Zipora Sasson
Sam Eisenstadt, 80
Victor Lashchiver
Yitzhak Rothenberg, 70
Yosef Zandani, 28
Asher Attia, 48
Vered Mordechai, 13
Maya Elharar, 17
Ilana Schreiber, 45
Meirav Ben-Moshe, 16
Ayala Vahaba, 40
Fadiya Shalabi, 25
Ahuva Cohen Onalla, 37
Yishai Gadassi, 32
Rahamim Mazgauker, 34
David Moyal, 26
Daga Perda, 44
Bilha Butin, 49
Sgt. Ari Perlmutter, 19
Shahar Simani, 20
Rafael Yairi Klumfenbert, 36

Margalit Ruth Shohat, 48
Staff Sgt. Moshe Bukra, 30
Cpl. Erez Ben-Baruch, 24
Sarit Prigal, 17
Arye Frankenthal, 20
Lt. Guy Ovadia, 23
BP Sgt.-Maj. Jacques Attias, 24
Yoram Sakuri, 30
Ron Soval, 18
Shlomo Kapach, 22
Gil Revah, 21
Sgt. Victor Shichman, 24
Natasha Ivanov, 32
Ma'ayan Levy, 19
Samir Mugrabi, 35
Cpl. Nahshon Wachsman, 20
Capt. Nir Poraz, 23
Haviv Tishbi, 54
Moshe Gardinger, 83
Pnina Rapaport, 74
Galit Rosen, 23
Zippora Ariel, 64
David Lida, 74
Puah Yedgar, 56
Dalia Ashkenazi, 62
Aviv Esther Sharon, 21
Ofra Ben-Naim, 33
Tamar Karlibach-Sapir, 24
Shira Meroz-Kot, 20
Miriam Adaf, 54
Anat Rosen, 21
Salah Ovadia, 52
Eliahu Wasserman, 66
Alexandra Sapirstein, 55
Dr. Pierre Atlas, 56
Ella Volkov, 21
Ayelet Langer-Alkobi, 26
Kochava Biton, 59
Rinier Yurest, 23
Capt. Yehazkel Sapir, 36
Lt. Yotam Rahat, 31
Capt. Elad Dror, 24
Sgt.-Maj. Gil Dadon, 26
Rabbi Amiran Olami, 34

Sgt. Liat Gabai, 19

1993
Yigal Vaknin
Dror Forer
Aran Bachar
Staff Sgt. (res) Ehud Rot, 35
Sgt. Ilan Levi, 23
Chaim Mizrahi
Efraim Ayubi
Salman Id el-Hawashla, 38
Sgt. 1st Cl. Chaim Darina, 37
Shalva Ozana, 23
Yitzhak Weinstock, 19
David Mashrati
Mordechai Lapid
Shalom Lapid, 19
Eliahu Levin
Meir Mendelovitch
Anatoly Kolisnikov
Chaim Weizman
David Bizi
Lieut. Col. Meir Mintz

Maps Of The Size And Borders Of Israel Since 1920

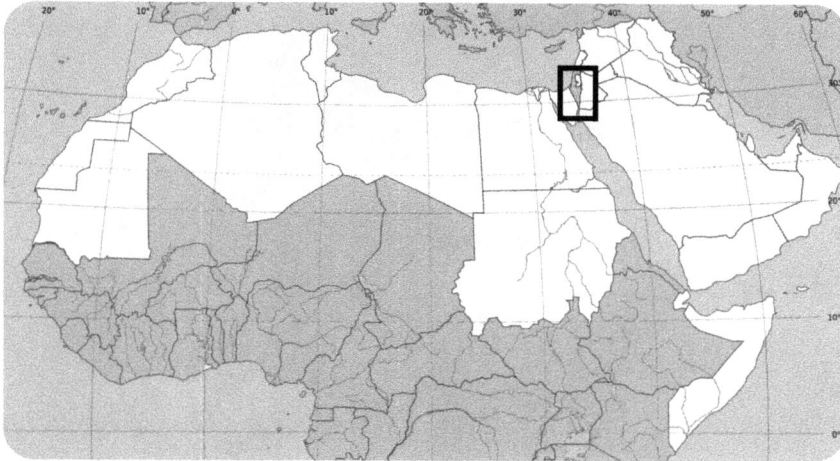

Israel's geographic size in comparison to the Arab countries.

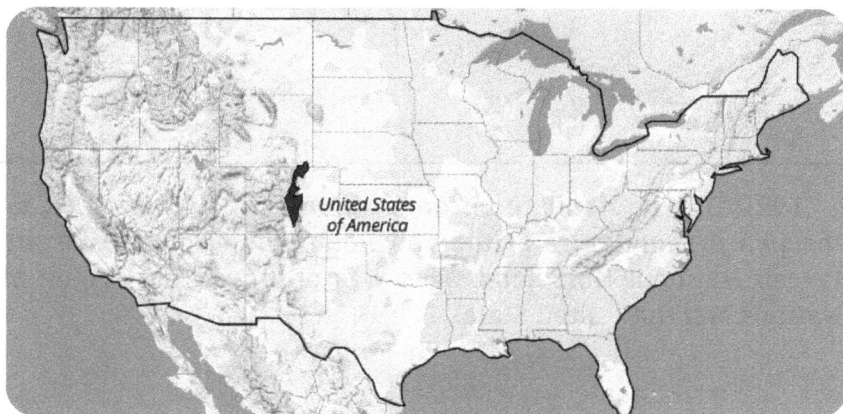

This to-scale map shows a size comparison of Israel compared to United States. Israel is approximately 21,937 sq km, while United States is approximately 9,833,517 sq km. Source: https://www.mylifeelsewhere.com/country-size-comparison/ united-states/israel

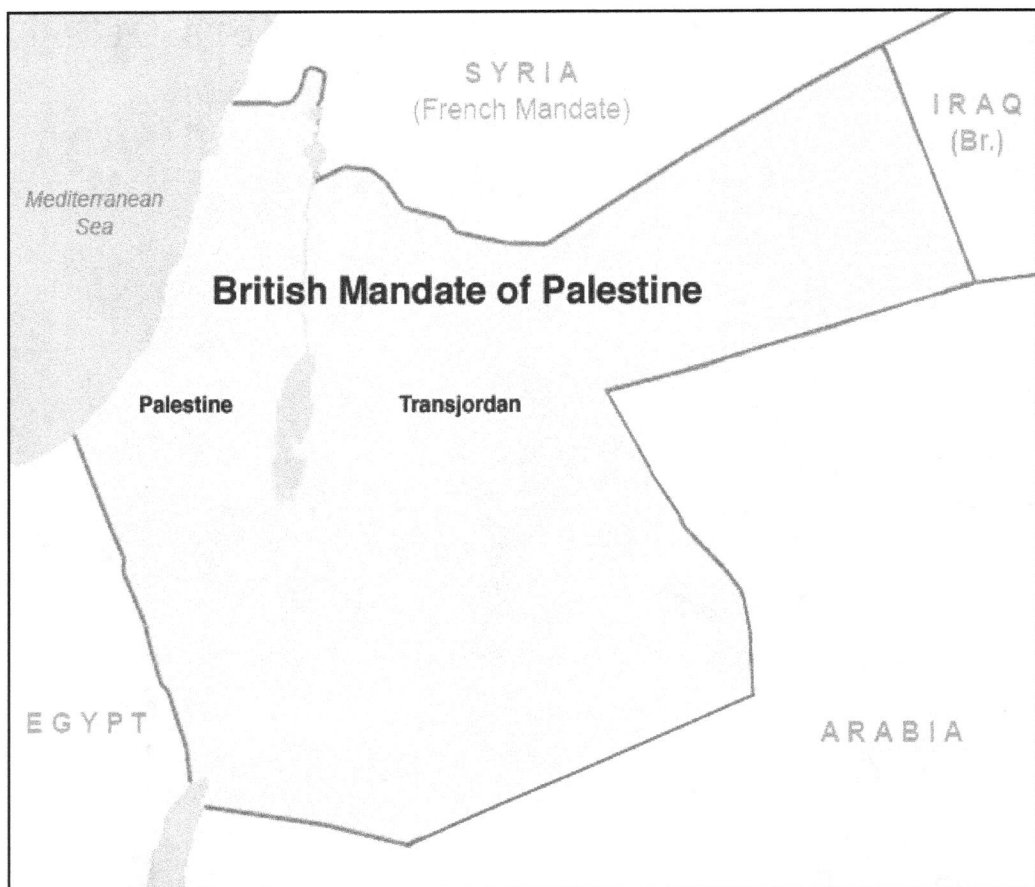

British Mandate of Palestine

SYRIA
(French Mandate)

IRAQ
(Br.)

Mediterranean
Sea

Palestine   Transjordan

EGYPT   ARABIA

1920 British Mandate borders for Palestine established by the peace negotiators at the San Remo conference to be the Jewish National Homeland. This was approved by League of Nations and the United States.

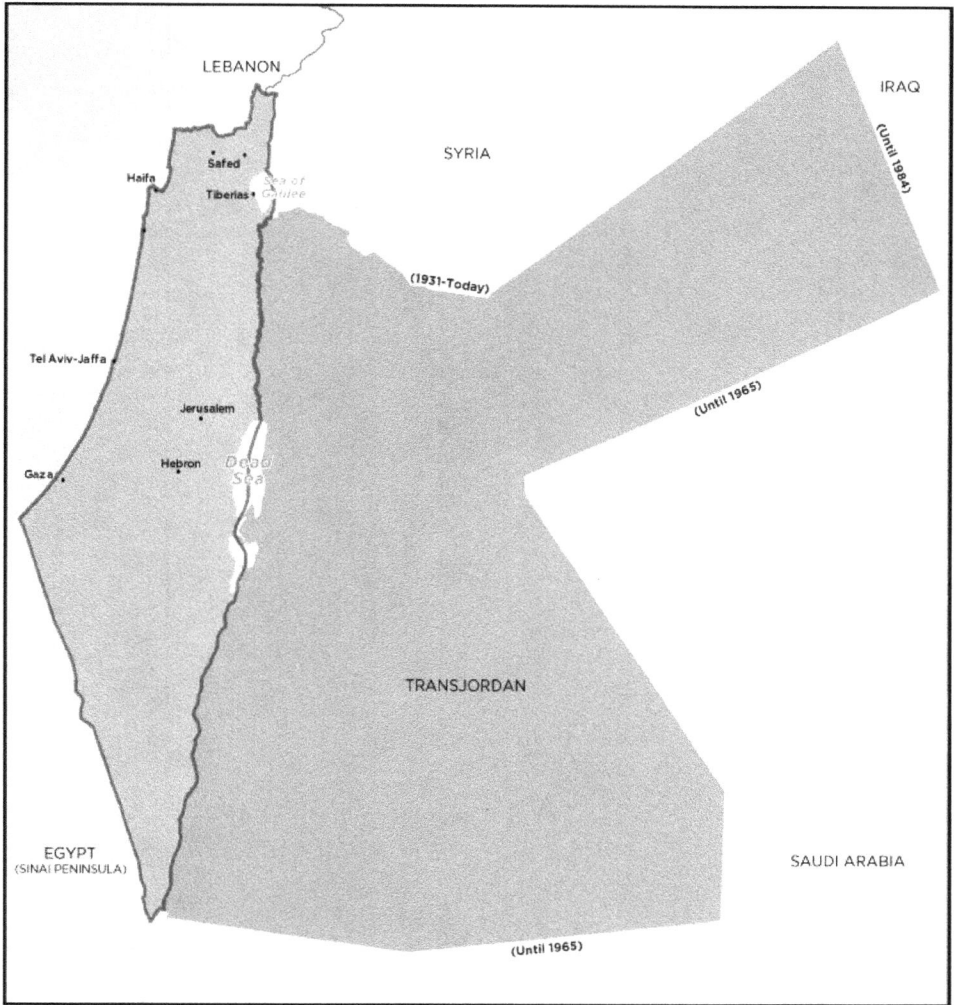

LEBANON

IRAQ

SYRIA

Safed

(Until 1984)

Haifa

Tiberias

Sea of
Galilee

(1931-Today)

Tel Aviv-Jaffa

Jerusalem

(Until 1965)

Hebron

Dead
Sea

Gaza

TRANSJORDAN

EGYPT
(SINAI PENINSULA)

SAUDI ARABIA

(Until 1965)

This map shows the division of land that ripped away from the Jews all of the lands east of the Jordan and created a new Arab country called Jordan, a British protectorate.

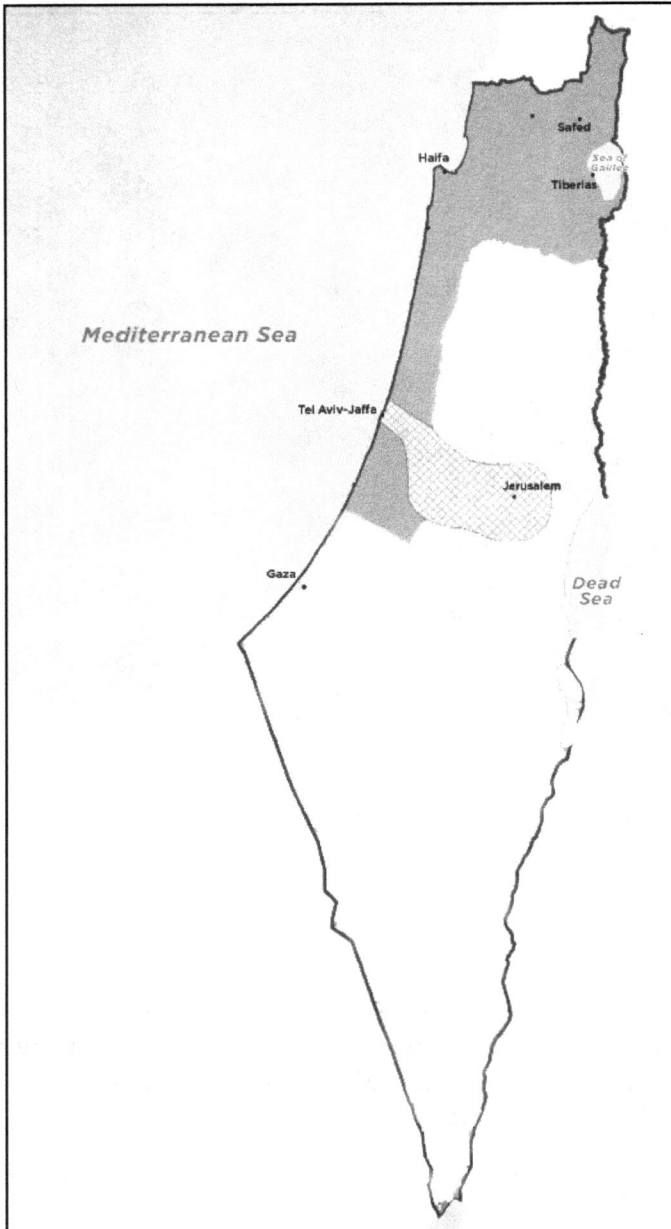

The proposed Peel Commission plan, within the outline, for partitioning a Jewish state (dark area), an Arab state (white area) and Jerusalem as an international zone (crisscross area), 1937. This partition was accepted by the Jews, but rejected by the Arabs.

The 1947 United Nations map showing their plan for partitioning a Jewish state, an Arab state and Jerusalem. The Arabs rejected the second compromise as well, preferring calls for genocide.

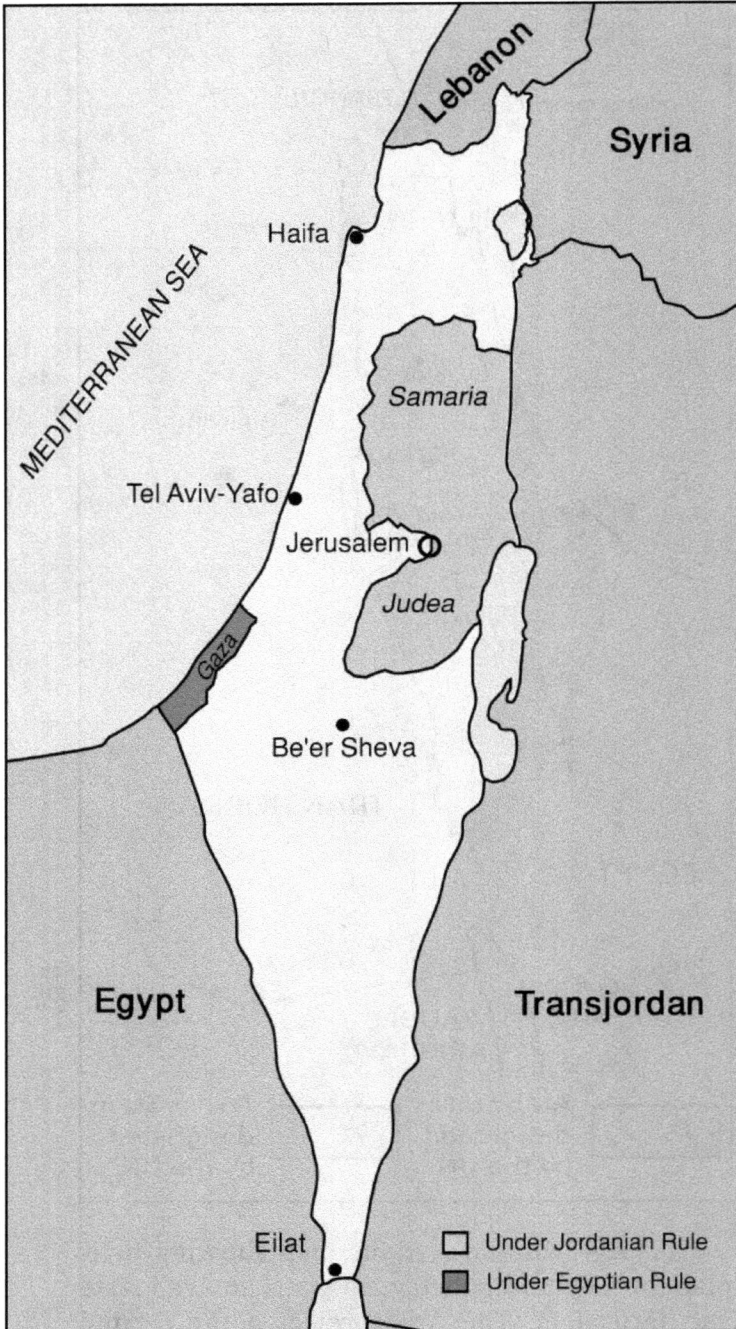

1949 Borders of Israel. Israel expanded beyond the partition plan (rejected by the Arabs) as a result of the war of genocide the Arabs launched and lost.

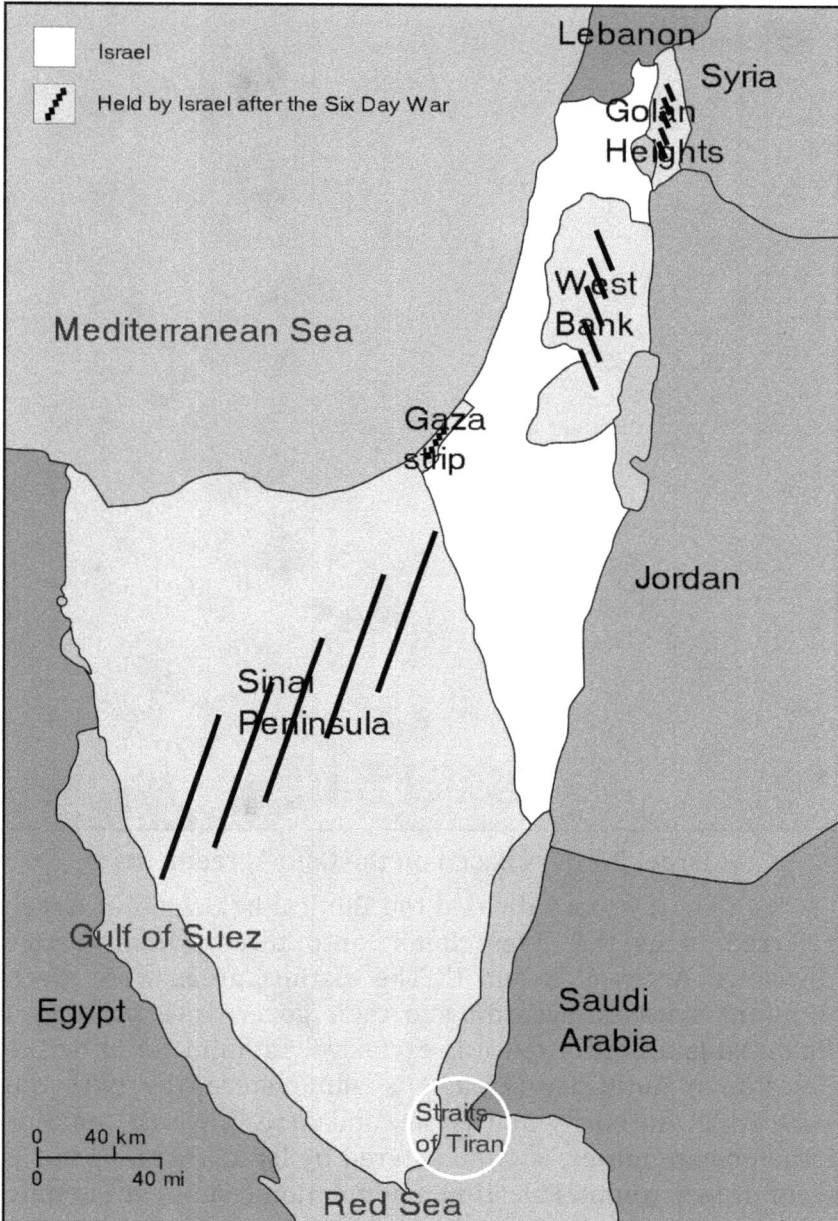

After the 1967 Six-Day War, Israel had captured the Sinai Peninsula, Gaza strip, West Bank and Golan Heights. Map Source: Wikipedia, Rafy-Six_Day_War_Terrritories map. Result of another war of genocide the Arabs launched and lost.

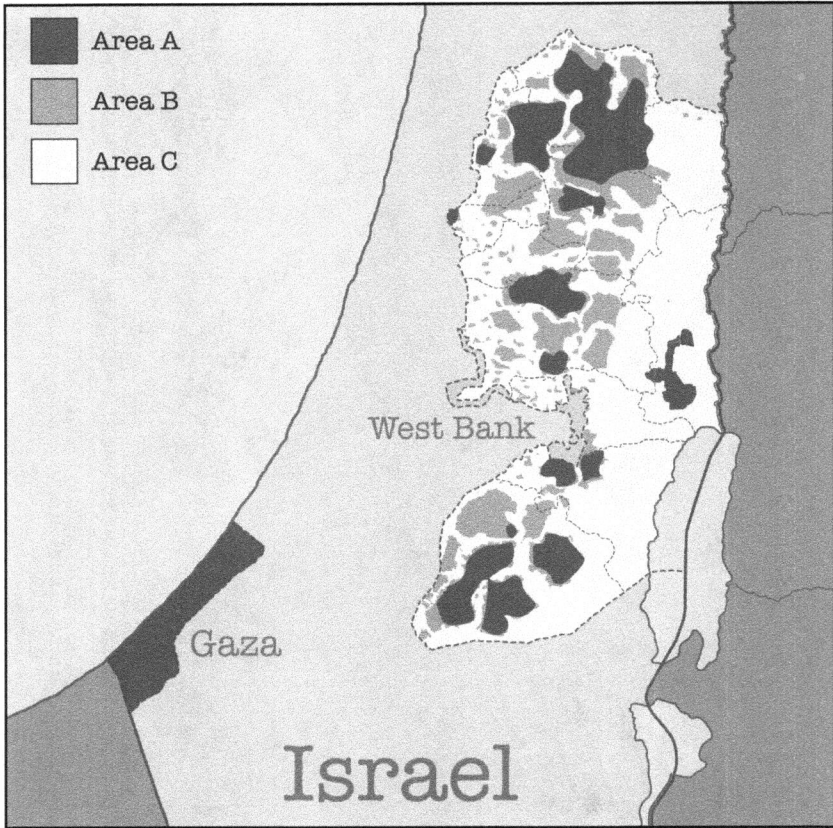

Israel Borders based on the Oslo Agreements

The Oslo II Accord divided the Biblical heartland of Israel, referred to as the "West Bank," into three administrative divisions: Areas A, B and C. The distinct areas were given different statuses, according to their governance pending a final status accord: Area A is exclusively administered by the Palestinian Authority; Area B is administered by both the Palestinian Authority and Israel; and Area C, which contains Israeli communities, is administered by Israel. Areas A and B were drawn around Palestinian population centers at the time the agreement was signed; all areas surrounding Areas A and B were defined as Area C.

Israel ceded critical parts of its Biblical heartland to Yassar Arafat's Palestine Liberation Organization in the hope of being granted peace in return.

The Author

Shalom Pollack was born in Brooklyn, New York, to an Orthodox family of teachers and rabbis. His father, Rabbi Baruch Pollack, taught first grade in yeshivot for sixty-one years.

Shalom graduated MTJ Yeshiva high school and went on to earn an MA in International Relations from Brooklyn College. The one year in Hebrew University in 1973-74, the year of the Yom Kippur War, was a major factor in his decision to make Aliyah in 1977.

Upon making Aliyah, he worked as a print and radio journalist before becoming a professional tour guide in 1980.

Much of his writing is inspired by the places he has come to know intimately and the varied people he guides in four languages.

Shalom served in the IDF reserves for ten years. The unique experiences there were invaluable to his understanding of Israeli society.

www.ingramcontent.com/pod-product-compliance
Lightning Source LLC
Chambersburg PA
CBHW072133270326
41931CB00010B/1749